Triumphing over Hell on Earth

Triumphing over Hell on Earth

Dr. Juniace Sénécharles Etienne

All Rights Reserved 2015 by Dr. Juniace Sénécharles Etienne

Cover and Graphics Design by: Trevor Pryce

No part of this book may be reproduced or transmitted in any forms or by any means, graphic, electronic, or mechanical, including photocopying, recording, taping, internet, or by any information storage retrieved system, without written permission of the publisher, Mavericks Press.

All Scripture quotations, unless otherwise indicated, are taken from the Holy Bible, New International Version®, NIV®. Copyright ©1973, 1978, 1984, 2011 by Biblica, Inc.™ Used by permission of Zondervan. All rights reserved worldwide. The "NIV" and "New International Version" are trademarks registered in the United States Patent and Trademark Office by Biblica, Inc.™

Maverick Press 2015

ISBN: 978-0-9965392-4-1

Printed in the United States of America
First Edition Printed: December, 2015

TABLE OF CONTENTS

DEDICATION 7
AKNOWLEDGEMENTS 9
INTRODUCTION 11
Chapter 1 - DO NOT WORRY ABOUT FOOD 21
Chapter 2 - DO NOT WORRY ABOUT WATER 33
Chapter 3 - WHAT SHOULD YOU WEAR 45
Chapter 4 - SHELTER 55
Chapter 5 - WHAT IS THE KINGDOM OF GOD? 63
Chapter 6 - WHAT IS GOD'S RIGHTEOUNESS? 71
Chapter 7 - HOW TO ENTER THE KINGDOM OF GOD 79
Chapter 8 - HOW TO DESCRIBE THE KINGDOM OF GOD 93
Chapter 9 - SELF-DISCOVERY 95
Chapter 10 - PLANNING 101
Chapter 11 - HOW TO WRITE YOUR VISION 111
Chapter 12 - TIME FOR A CHANGE 117
APPENDIX 134
Recommended Readings 135
About the Author 136
Other Works by the Author 137

DEDICATION

This book is dedicated to:

- Dr. Myles Munroe, who had devoted his entire life to teaching the Kingdom Message to the world. I miss him so much...

- Trista Sue Kragh, who not only teaches the Kingdom Message but teaches me how to live a Kingdom Life Style. Thank you for teaching about purpose and vision and your dedication to each leader of the Kingdom Community International in Naples, Florida and various nations.

- Pastor Lori Michelle Snell, who has taught me how to be a believer.

- To my daughters Joyce and Jessica Gayo, Samantha and Sheena Etienne. May your potential be maximized in your generation.

- To the entire Sénécharles and Etienne family, and more specifically to all my nieces and nephews. May your potential be maximized in your generation.

AKNOWLEDGEMENTS

I am honored to acknowledge the following people who helped with the development and production of this vision:

My dear husband, Romel Etienne, for your patience and support during the writing process of this vision. Thank you for your encouraging words.

Cathy Keeler, for your great devotion, your kindness, and your willingness to embrace the idea my vision is worth sharing with the world. I appreciate every second, every minute, and every hour you spent editing this book. Thank you for allowing the King to use your gift as my resource to accomplish His will through me.

Howard Howell, thank you for your input and support.

Debra Horner, thank you so much for your time and your expertise.

Sheena Etienne, thank you for your help, and your gift of researching.

And last but not least, my Kingdom Community, thank you for all the prayers and the support.

Triumphing Over Hell On Earth

INTRODUCTION

Food, water, clothing, and shelter are basic human needs, and highly needed to carry on with the daily routine of what we call "life" and living. These basic human needs are critically important for our well-being. They cannot be ignored because of the continuous reminder of the important role they may play in our lives, as well as the emphasis made by society on how we may not have enough of these simple basic human needs to carry on. There is a constant loud noise being played in our head. I call it a reminder. This loud voice constantly plays the same tune "more food, better water, larger houses, and bigger closets," and for some people the tune may be "you are starving, you have no access to clean water, you have no clothes, and by the way, your house is a dump." A prediction was made by our Creator that if we don't obtain these items the proper way we would lose our focus, our purpose, our self-worth, our abilities, our creativity, and our vision through the process of searching for them. If we continue to ignore the knowledge on how to properly obtain these basic needs we could lose our identity, because the resource is within us.

A Master Teacher was needed to be in place to teach us the principles, the skills, the strategies, and the keys on how to achieve these basic human needs on earth without losing ourselves. A Master Teacher was sent 2,000 plus years ago to teach us these skills and principles that you and I need. Because of our religious mindsets we tend to have a hard time understanding them and even a harder time applying them in our life.

Presently, many people work at least two jobs just to own these basic human needs, not realizing they can have total access of their Creator's resources available to them instead. This is because of the fall of man through disobedience of the Divine Laws and Principles. A promise of restoration was made by our Creator (God), and kept through His son Jesus Christ. He sent His son as a Master Teacher to teach us the way and to give us the keys to life. Food, water, clothing, shelter are the items about which many people are leaving their countries and risking their lives and their children's lives with the hope that one day they will be able to provide for their family. And for some people, if they don't leave their country on time, they may starve to death.

I, too, had to leave my country. My parents had the fear that Haiti may never regain its governmental stability due to lack of character and integrity of the authorities to meet the basic human needs of its people. My parents, being the kind of parents they are, felt the need to relocate the family. I came to realize that the safety nest they wanted to give me was already planned, was in place, and was within me to develop. Regardless of where I find myself, the plan stays the same. The responsibility lies on me, however, to seek the way, by understanding who I am; be in good standing; recognizing that I have a purpose; and to create a plan to achieve that purpose by utilizing the resources that I have on hand.

Living away from Haiti did not guarantee that I would have the basic human needs such as food, water, clothes, and shelter because there are a lot of people living in America who do not have access to these simple basic needs. This is why our Creator forbade us to measure our life

Introduction

success based on them **Matthew 6: 25** "Therefore I tell you, do not worry about your life, what you will eat or drink; or about your body, what you will wear. Is not life more than food, and the body more than clothes?"[1] It is demanded from us to disregard the emphasis made by the world about these basic human needs in order to avoid burying our thoughts into the process of just food, water, clothing, and shelter. Instead, we have to be reminded in whose image we were created. We are made in God's image. **Genesis 1:26** clarifies this statement for us, "Let us make mankind in our image, in our likeness, so that they may rule over the fish in the sea and the birds in the sky, over the livestock and all the wild animals, and over all the creatures that move along the ground."[2] We were given a kingdom, the dominion over earth, the ability to become ourselves with purpose and vision, because we have gifts and talents. This was and still is the foundation for our creation.

Yes, we were dislocated due to the fall of man but the purpose of that foundation remains the same, "dominion over earth." God sent His son to help us rediscover that purpose. **John 3: 16-17** "For God so loved the world that he gave His one and only Son, that whoever believes in him shall not perish but have eternal life. For God did not send his Son into the world to condemn the world, but to save the world through him."[3]

Jesus also came to teach us how to repent and how to transform our mindset in order to receive His kingdom and the benefits of the kingdom. In the kingdom there is no ownership. We have access to it all. I have learned that having access is the way to go. The truth is we all want access we just don't know how to differentiate between

---

1 Matthew 6: 25
2 Genesis 1:26
3 John 3: 16-17

access and ownership due to our democratic background culture.

This is a fundamental key for us to grasp because it will help us understand the navigation system needed to be utilized in order to regain control over who we are, or our identity. If you don't know your story, you can't move forward. Until you know who you are or where you came from, it would be almost impossible to find your identity. My parents moved me from Haiti to the United States and instilled in me that if I go to school, if I work hard in life, I will never be in need of these simple basic needs such as food, water, clothing, and shelter. That is the foundation they gave me.

My parents meant well, and I love them dearly. So I decided to obtain the highest degree: a doctorate. Yet the way to obtain simple basic human needs have not significantly changed. I used to work more than one job and still no major improvement. At times, I would feel as if I were running out of fuel just to make do. I was toiling, a method that does not exist for good standing kingdom citizens. The only thing that was clear to me was the fact that I did not want to be consumed by the thought of going through life just for "these items." Over the years I had narrowed my circle of people who had the mindset of just living for these items. I knew something had to be different but I was not sure of what it could be, but I learned to stay away from these people because my spirit was not at peace talking about having the latest shoes and latest designer handbag. That was not my "thing." But what was my "thing?"

I was always in church. I never felt church could give me the answer I was seeking. I did not always understand the process of going to church, but I was going. I wasn't thinking about the process. The truth is, in religion, you are not supposed to think. So with that religious mindset I wasn't

Introduction

supposed to think for myself, I never really understood the mission of Jesus, and the importance of commonwealth until now.

I was uncomfortable with the idea of worrying about simple basic needs. I was going to church, even praying about getting my basic human needs met while not knowing that I was using the wrong key (prayer) to open the wrong door (basic human needs). I did not know that understanding the kingdom is far more important than food, water, clothing and shelter. I was operating out of order, going against the plan that was in place for me.

I was functioning on my own human logical mindset, hoping that I could own my living. In essence, one of Jesus' mission was to caution me not to worry about these basic human needs and to instead place my focus on seeking God's Kingdom which holds the secret code and complete access of resources available to become myself, and for you to become yourselves as well.

The late Dr. Myles Munroe defines Kingdom as follows:

"The governing influence of a king over his territory, impacting it with his personal will, purpose, and intent, producing a culture, values, morals, and lifestyles that reflect the king's desires and nature for his citizens."

This book has several purposes. The first one is to help you rediscover what it means to live a lifestyle that reflects your king, a lifestyle that reflects the culture of purpose, the culture of character and integrity, and vision to accomplish the king's will here on earth with the resources that are provided to us. "Seek first His kingdom and His righteousness."[4] The purpose of this book is to also help you

---

[4] Matthew 6: 33

understand Jesus' teaching as eloquently stated in **Matthew 6: 25-30** "Therefore I tell you, do not worry about your life, what you will eat or drink; or about your body, what you will wear. Is not life more than food, and the body more than clothes? Look at the birds of the air; they do not sow or reap or store away in barns, and yet your heavenly Father feeds them. Are you not much more valuable than they? Can any one of you by worrying add a single hour to your life? "And why do you worry about clothes? See how the flowers of the field grow. They do not labor or spin. Yet I tell you that not even Solomon in all his splendor was dressed like one of these. If that is how God clothes the grass of the field, which is here today and tomorrow is thrown into the fire, will he not much more clothe you—you of little faith?"[5]

My parents had moved me out of Haiti to the United States with the fear that Haiti's government, due to their lack of character and integrity, would hinder my chance of becoming self-sufficient. My parents did not want me to worry about simple basic human needs. They felt it was out of their hands because I was created for a purpose, and as a result, the resources needed to accomplish my purpose were established by my Creator.

Later, I found myself repeating the same steps as my parents. This time, not moving my children from one country to another, but instilling in them the same value that if they got the "right education" and worked hard they would never have to worry about simple basic human needs. I was passing down to them what I had learned from my parents. I must say, my daughters are a lot smarter than me, because they understand something that I never knew: Purpose. They understand that if they are operating according to their purpose with the right planning, they will never be in need of

---

[5]Matthew 6:25-30

Introduction

basic human needs, because they will be functioning in Divine Laws and Principles according to their Creator.

Through these words I hope that you regain your purpose, your vision, and develop a plan. I hope you rediscover your gifts, your talents, your creativity, your ability, and your capacity, regardless of what you have been told in the past. I hope to give you some applicable principles you may be able to use to supplement your lifestyle's culture, to start your journey, or to simply take the first step to a "Self-discovery" process to better your environment, your community, the third world nations and people with a third world mentality.

In the worst case, I hope these pages serve the purpose to help you understand that you are important, you are meaningful, you are able to make changes because you were purposefully created by your Creator with a very specific assignment that only you can do. People may imitate your task but they will never be able to accomplish it with the same ability and passion because they would be operating out of order. That passion you have in your heart is yours no matter how much you want to move away from it. It keeps coming back in your mind. This is God communicating with you through the Holy Spirit. Don't ignore that voice. He is trying to get your attention because He has an assignment for your life, "May His will be done on earth just like it is in heaven"[6] through each one of us who understands our purpose and live the lifestyle that reflects the King's Divine Laws and Principles here on earth.

Three years ago, I could not even imagine that I would be writing a book that could help you understand that your life means more than just working for food, water, clothing, and shelter. I was very content with my life by raising my

---

[6] Matthew 6:10

Triumphing Over Hell On Earth

children and enjoying teaching my students. Trista Sue Kragh, my mentor, helped me understand that in the kingdom people don't just go with the motion. People have a plan because they understand that they have a purpose. They make their vision a reality by identifying their gifts and talents to serve the world. You are full of resources. Look around and start with what you have. The rest will come later. I am still a teacher, but now I understand that my purpose is bigger than just teaching. I was born to shape young people's minds so they can discover their purpose for their education which will save them time, money, and energy and of course be better prepared to solve the problem of basic human needs: food, water, clothing, and shelter.

I understand that my purpose is to provide resources to third world leaders to help them transform their educational system by developing purposefully minded teachers to help students find in return their purpose to transform their country by removing that third world label and replacing it with a progressive world. Maya Angelou once said, "If you find it in your heart to care for somebody else, you will have succeeded." It is the culture of the kingdom for the king to provide for his citizens. **Romans 14:17** "For the kingdom of God is not a matter of eating and drinking, but of righteousness, peace and joy in the Holy Spirit." [7] It is therefore in my culture to duplicate the principles, and the keys to life that I have learned through my mentors Dr. Myles Munroe and Sue Kragh. This process is called "Pass it on." When you have it, you must pass it forward. It is like "yeast", it has to multiply. **Luke 13: 33** explained, "The kingdom of heaven is like yeast that a woman took and mixed into about sixty pounds of flour until it worked all through the dough."[8] I am in the process of helping others understand

---

7 Romans 14:17

8 Luke 13: 33

Introduction

what I have learned and how my life has transformed when I made the decision to "seek the kingdom and His righteousness."[9]

The term kingdom is referring to "the sovereign rule of a king over his territory (domain), to impact it with his will, purpose, and intent." The definition of kingdom from the bible's perspective is "God's government, God's rulership, God's dominion over the earth." According to Dr. Munroe "The kingdom of God means God's will executed, God's jurisdiction, Heaven's influence, God's administration, and God's impact and influence." This is what my seeking is all about.

The term righteousness comes from the discipline of law. It has nothing to do with religion. It means right standing. In order for you and I to be righteous we have to be in alignment with authority. We have to be in right positioning with authority, and we have to have correct fellowship with authority. We have to fulfill all the requirements of authority. Similarly, if I want to exercise my rights as a citizen of the United States, I have to be in good standing with the law, otherwise my rights may be revoked by the authority. If I want to remain a safe driver, I have to respect the laws of the department of the motor vehicles. The key is I have to follow the laws in order to receive the benefits of my county and the benefits of the kingdom as well.

---

9 Matthew 6:10

Key Principles:
1. Resources are within you.
2. Know who you are.
3. Understand that you have a purpose.
4. You have gifts and talents.
5. Transformation must be made in order to receive the kingdom.
6. Your lifestyle must reflect your belief system.

Chapter 1

DO NOT WORRY ABOUT FOOD

"For the kingdom of God is not a matter of eating and drinking, but of righteousness, peace and joy in the Holy Spirit."[10]

What is Food?

The first lesson taught by the Master Teacher: Do not worry about food. His essential question was "Can any one of you by worrying add a single hour to your life?"[11]

As a child I weighed very little because I was not into eating. I was always feeling too lazy to eat. I remember I would see the food, I would want to eat it but my mind was feeling too lazy to go through the process of chewing. When they would ask me why I did not eat my food my answer was, "I don't want to chew and swallow the food, too much work!" In my mind it was an unbearable process, so I would not eat. If I were living in America, I would have been diagnosed as having some type of eating disorder. I am not sure which because anorexia has to do with weight loss and I was definitely not concerned about my weight. Bulimia has

---

10 Romans 14:17
11 Matthew 6:27

to do with extreme overeating, also known as binging, definitely not me. I am happy to say, presently, I enjoy my food and the process of eating because food is a very important substance that we consume in order to receive the necessary nutritional elements that our bodies need to function properly. Food can be plant-based or animal-based. We receive our energy through the consumption of the right amount of food that we eat. For example, we receive our energy through food because it has vitamins, minerals, fats, and proteins.

Through food we can have life, and we can grow. Food can also be a killer agent through obesity when too much of it is consumed or malnutrition when not enough is taken. Food has always been important for us as humans. In my case it was different. I am still unsure of the reason I felt that way toward eating. Ten thousand years ago, we used the method of hunting, gathering, and agriculture to secure our food. We would spend hours and hours in hiding hoping we would be fortunate to kill an animal or fish to feed our family. The process of hunting was very harsh because it was done from a distance from home regardless of the season and the weather conditions. We used to gather wild fruit and berries, nuts, and vegetables to supplement our diet.

Presently, we use a more sophisticated and rapid system in order to meet the high food demands to produce a sufficient amount of food to feed everyone.

What is the Impact of Food on Earth?

As the population increases, so does the demand of food supply. The earth is getting to be very crowded as many of us can see within our neighborhood, within our community, within our school system, and basically everywhere. The global population is over 7 billion people. According to research, it is increasing by "78 million people

Do Not Worry About Food

per year." It is predicted the earth's population will rise up to 8 billion people by 2027 and about 9 billion by 2046. What does that mean for the food chain? It means "scarcity" according to the economists. We have to develop more proficient hormones so the chickens can lay more eggs per day, and the tomato harvest needs to reoccur more often.

I remember when I was in Haiti during the month of April, 2015 I saw mangoes all over the streets being sold by the street merchants and I asked the taxi driver "Is it mango season?" His answer was "No, there is no such thing as mango season, we produce mango all year long to supply the demands of other countries that buy from us." And he said, "We have to use a lot of fertilizer to make the mango trees produce all year long." I was astonished because I remember that growing up in Haiti summer was always fun because it was mango season, the time my brothers and I would go visit my grandmother, Viergelie Sanon. We would stay up all night eating mango and my grandmother would be telling us stories of the past. Now we have to produce more food, and make the trees produce out of their season to meet the high demands of food supply with the hope of feeding all seven plus billion people on earth. **Ecclesiastes 3:1** tells us "There is a time for everything, and a season for every activity under the heavens."[12] We are operating the land out of order, against its season. The ability to feed seven plus billion people on earth was never an issue for God. He provided us with the necessary means to cultivate the lands and He created us with skills and abilities to develop innovative ideas and concepts that are essential to produce the food within order.

God is not surprised at all that we are troubled with the idea of feeding seven plus billion people. I would say He may be frustrated by the way we choose to disregard the

---

[12]Ecclesiastes 3:1

Triumphing Over Hell On Earth

perfect identity He gave us and we live life contrary to the plan that He created for us. He is perhaps heart-broken by the philosophy we choose to adapt to justify our misdoings, to process and analyze things differently from His original plan that He had for us. Regrettably, we have it all wrong, because we are doing it our way instead of just simply following His perfect plan. **Genesis 1:26** clearly explains how He made us and His perfect plan that He had for us, "Let us make mankind in our image, in our likeness, so that they may rule over the fish in the sea and the birds in the sky, over the livestock and all the wild animals, and over all the creatures that move along the ground."[13]

We were created in God's image, meaning we have His ability, His capacity, His character, His creativity, and His power to dominate and control our environment with proper order. God also designed our lives to be lived with high standards and with the prosperity with all that we do.

Genesis 1:28 God blessed them and said to them, "Be fruitful and increase in number; fill the earth and subdue it. Rule over the fish in the sea and the birds in the sky and over every living creature that moves on the ground."[14] God ordained us to rule and He gave us ownership over the earth. God gave us all the food we would need to take care of ourselves from generation to generation, but we have to manage it properly.

Genesis 1: 29-30 Then God said, "I give you every seed-bearing plant on the face of the whole earth and every tree that has fruit with seed in it. They will be yours for food. And to all the beasts of the earth and all the birds in the sky and all the creatures that move along the ground—everything that has the breath of life in it—I give every green plant for

---

[13] Genesis 1:26
[14] Genesis 1: 28

Do Not Worry About Food

food."[15] That was His plan, His food bank for us, His pantry, His deep-freezer, His grocery store for us.

Unfortunately, that plan failed because of the fall of man through disobedience. We lost the kingdom and all the benefits that came with the kingdom. **Genesis 3: 17** "Cursed is the ground because of you; through painful toil you will eat food from it all the days of your life."[16] We are still enduring the impact of the fall of man. We see the result of mismanagement.

God loves us so much that He decided to restore that plan into place. He understood that we had a hard time learning and applying His original plan. He ordained His son Jesus Christ as a Master Teacher to come to earth and reinstruct us about His original plan, how to rediscover ourselves and to regain access to the kingdom that we once lost due to disobedience, and learn how to manage what we have.

It is told that from the very beginning Jesus only taught one lesson "The Kingdom" which was His mission, His Father's goal and objective, His mandate from His Heavenly Father to restore the kingdom of God on earth that man had lost. Dr. Munroe stated that, "Mankind's failure through disobedience to his Creator resulted in the loss of his dominion over the earth." Since we lost the kingdom and its benefits we are having difficulty meeting our basic human needs such as food. How do we feed seven plus billion people? Where would we get the skills to work the land? How can we design tractors that can work all over the earth, not just in well-developed countries, but in third world countries as well? How can we make the land more fertile? Why are people leaving their country just to be fed? We are

---

[15] Genesis 1: 29-30
[16] Genesis 3: 17

Triumphing Over Hell On Earth

talking about basic human needs. This is what Jesus had to say about this matter.

Matthew 6: 25 "Therefore I tell you, do not worry about your life, what you will eat or drink; or about your body, what you will wear. Is not life more than food, and the body more than clothes?"[17]

It is clearly stated that we should not have to worry about what we are going to eat, because our lives do not depend on food alone. According to God, that should not be a concern at all because He had already designed a plan. He promised us His kingdom since the very beginning, and we should never have to worry about where our next meal is coming from. We should never have to be concerned about how many harvests of corn we should have during the year. God knew it was going to be a problem, however. He knew it because He created us and He knows what the human body needs to receive the necessary energy in order to maintain the proper balance. He knows that we need the vitamins, minerals, fats, and proteins. He knows that if we don't have enough greens and vegetables on our plate our bodies will be deficient and yet He tells us not to even think about food because the needed resources are in placed.

As you may know we are not the only creation of God. He created all the resources that we need. He thought about everything on earth, I mean everything: the fish, the birds, the plants, and the oceans. Basically He gave us a food bank. **Genesis 1:29** Then God said, "I give you every seed-bearing plant on the face of the whole earth and every tree that has fruit with seed in it. They will be yours for food."[18]

---

[17] Matthew 6: 25
[18] Genesis 1: 29

Do Not Worry About Food

And He gave us access to them. He knew what we would be in need of, so He provided everything before you and I were even born.

Because He understands our mindsets so well, He knew we would show signs of concern or demonstrate a lack of faith about the source of the food supply. Because we tend to forget who our original source is, He decided to give us examples of His other creations who are able to eat on time, never miss a meal and yet they don't even have to work. Jesus said if you don't believe me go, outside and look at the birds of the air, do they have a farm? Do you see them working? Are they stressing where their next meal is coming from? Absolutely not! As a matter of fact, they don't even "sow or reap or store away in barns..." Jesus is telling us these birds don't have a deep-freezer, they don't have a pantry, yet they receive their food on time daily. He tells us, if I am your father and their father why would I meet their food needs and not yours? So, go again outside and watch them in action. Everything is provided for them. If I can do it for them, I can do it for you too. Just trust me. You have no faith. If you want to receive the kingdom and its benefits that I promised, you have to stop worrying about your next meal. The worries can hinder your ability to see the bigger picture. The worries can paralyze your capacity to move forward.

You cannot be in the prayer line thinking about what you are going to feed your family because last time you took an inventory of your pantry it was empty. Now you are panicking. Please don't be "afraid" and "If your heavenly Father feeds them are you not much more valuable than they?"[19] The truth is, if we are not careful, the devil will use food as an incentive to get us on his team. We are not better than Jesus. He tempted Jesus with food. Fortunately, Jesus was and is a good Son. He remembered that his Father

---
19 Matthew 6:26

Triumphing Over Hell On Earth

told Him not to worry about food, because it is not all that we need to make in life. This is how Jesus was tested according to **Matthew 4:2-4.2** "After fasting forty days and forty nights, he was hungry. The tempter came to him and said, "If you are the Son of God, tell these stones to become bread. Jesus answered, "It is written: 'Man shall not live on bread alone, but on every word that comes from the mouth of God."[20]

Temptation is real, but we have to welcome it because it shows our true character when we pass the test. Raising my children as a single mother I must say I too was tested, but I did not know that then. I am happy to say I did pass the test. My twin daughters and I would go to Wednesday night service. The routine was for us to go to an affordable dinner before service. Although the places we would go were inexpensive, I did not always have the funds to pay for it. So I would pretend that my daughters were a lot younger than they were so I could pay the child's price. The cashiers would not have noticed because the girls were very petite and still are, but I knew that I was lying, even worse, I was teaching my daughters how to lie, which is terrible. One particular Wednesday night, when the funds were once again low, I was in line ready to go through the motion one more time. Quickly, I realized what I was doing. Now that I know better,

I would say the Holy Spirit was talking to me and asking me what was I doing in line knowing as a fact that I was about to pretend. I stopped and told my girls, "Put the trays away, we are not going to eat." They asked, "Why?" I said, "I don't have enough money to pay for our meal." I continued, "By the way girls, please forgive me and my behavior, I had no business bringing you to the restaurant knowing that I did not have enough money. What I was

---

[20]Matthew 4:2-4

Do Not Worry About Food

about to do is wrong and I know I have done this in the past. I am very sorry. It will never happen again. From now on if I don't have enough money we will stay home and eat whatever we have at home." I applause my obedience for listening to the Holy Spirit because this is the time the would devil go happy, had I not followed the voice of my King.

The devil will seize the moment when your children are starving and, as a parent, you won't know how you will be able to feed them. The devil will tease your eyes with food. That is why you have to train your eyes to be able to "see more than they can look." What I mean by that is you have to be able to look at your children straight in the eyes and say "Yes the pantry is empty, yes mom and dad are not able to feed you like your friends are being fed, but trust me our God said not to worry about food. Instead, let us pray for an idea how to create food. Let's petition our Creator to open our eyes to find the solution that can solve this hunger problem. Let's ask Him to show us our culinary creativity in the kitchen so we can transform this packet of Ramen Noodles into a gourmet meal." Faith and creativity go hand and hand. Growing up in a big family, my mother had to be very creative to feed us all. I remember when she was cooking rice she would ask all of us to puff our mouth until the rice was cooked. Later on, I learned that was a way to multiply each grain of rice being cooked in the pot. Miraculously, the amount would increase.

What I know for sure is we always had enough rice to eat, because of her faith and her creativity. This routine was very common in my community where I grew up in Haiti. As you can see it doesn't matter where we are, we may be in need of food. My parents had moved me away from Haiti, because in their minds they wanted to eliminate the fear of growing up in a country hindered in becoming self-sufficient. They could never imagine living in America. I would still need to apply and follow the Divine Laws and Principles in order to receive the keys to life. They did their part as parents. I learned that I too have to take responsibility, which comes with ability. I am responsible to learn the keys to life that are available to me so I can understand my ability to manage and to protect what I have been trusted with, Divine Laws and principles to life on earth.

Matthew 6:26 "Look at the birds of the air; they do not sow or reap or store away in barns, and yet your heavenly Father feeds them. Are you not much more valuable than they?"[21]

There are many people dying of hunger everyday especially in third world countries. They can't seem to find enough food to eat because they can't seem to find the right irrigation method, and there is a lack of fertilization to pollinate their lands. The educational system can't seem to develop and produce good enough agronomists who can study their land to make the right recommendation. They can't seem to produce great mechanical tools to work the land.

God equipped us with all that we need inside of us to be self-sufficient. Sometimes we are worried about things that are unnecessary just like Martha did in the Bible. She was so preoccupied with preparing food for Jesus, although Jesus never told her that He was hungry. She took it upon herself and yet she got upset because her sister was not helping out.

This is how Luke explained the story to us:

"As Jesus and his disciples were on their way, he came to a village where a woman named Martha opened her home to him. She had a sister called Mary, who sat at the Lord's

---
[21] Matthew 6:26

Do Not Worry About Food

feet listening to what He said. But Martha was distracted by all the preparations that had to be made. She came to Him and asked, "Lord, don't you care that my sister has left me to do the work by myself? Tell her to help me!" "Martha, Martha," the Lord answered, "You are worried and upset about many things, but few things are needed—or indeed only one. Mary has chosen what is better, and it will not be taken away from her."[22]

What are you preoccupied with? Are you following your Creator's instruction to make yourself eligible to receive His kingdom? Are you stressing over your next meal? God is a God of truth, He says " not to worry" not even the birds are worried about their next meal. **Romans 14:17** "For the kingdom of God is not a matter of eating and drinking, but of righteousness, peace and joy in the Holy Spirit."[23] Why are you slowing the process?

The day I made the decision not to lie about my daughters' ages just to feed them was the day blessings started pouring my way. I remember I had a client who brought me a bag of groceries with all that I would need to prepare many meals. I was so shocked because I did not see it coming. As a matter of fact she and I never talked about food and groceries before. She told me "I went to the store today, a sale was going on so I decided to do your groceries as well." I had a hard time accepting her offer at the time. Now that I am reflecting on it, I understand that I had activated several keys to life: first the key of obedience. I walked out of the restaurant. Second, I went home and cooked dinner using the groceries I had. I don't remember what I cooked but I am sure that it was good, because I don't recall any complaints from the girls.

---

22 Luke 10: 38-42
23 Romans 14:17

Key Principles

1. Seek first His kingdom and His righteousness.
2. Have faith.
3. Believe that you have the ability to receive what you want in life.
4. Pray for ideas, not for food.
5. Have a plan.
6. Have a vision for your life and your community.
7. Don't engross your mind with unnecessary projects, instead seek Him for ideas.

Chapter 2

DO NOT WORRY ABOUT WATER

Water is Everywhere and Everything

"Therefore I tell you, do not worry about your life, what you will eat or drink; or about your body, what you will wear. Is not life more than food, and the body more than clothes?"[24]

The second lesson taught by the Master Teacher: Do not worry about water. His essential question was the same, "Can any one of you by worrying add a single hour to your life?"[25]

God created the earth with a purpose and for a purpose including the water system. God created it with a very specific purpose. The purpose of this hydration system by our Creator was to meet our water needs. He puts in place Divine Laws and Principles to protect us from abusing its purpose.

The purpose of why water was created is extremely important to life. Its purpose becomes vital for all known forms of life on earth. We cannot live without it. Water is a

---

24 Matthew 6:25
25 Matthew 6:27

must for all of us: humans, plants, and animals. How do we use water? We need water to drink. We need it to keep our bodies clean, to bathe, and to wash our hands. We need water to cook. We need water to wash our dishes, and to wash our clothes. We need it to nourish our plants. We basically need water for almost everything. If water is so important how can we afford not worry about it? Better yet, do you think our heavenly Father doesn't know that water is that important to us? If there were no water, people and animals would go thirsty and quickly die. Even the plants would die without water. Yet our Father who created us in His "likeness" made it His business to tell us in advance not to let the fear of not having water become an issue or concern. Rather, He wants us to obey, respect, and apply the Divine Laws, and the Principles that He put in place to protect the purpose of water. These Divine Laws and Principles are locked into the two prerequisites: first "seek the Kingdom" and second "His righteousness."

We were also created with a purpose and for a purpose. Before we were born, the Creator knew us and He knows all we would need to have access to in order to accomplish His mandate (purpose) that He sent us to accomplish on earth. For tools, He gave us dominion, time, ability, passion, desire, and authority to accomplish the tasks that are hidden inside of us.

Process of Creation

Before God created us He created the earth with 71% of its surface covered with water. Later on, he created us. He made our body with a high percentage of water. Yet, God predicted the distribution of drinkable water would be an issue since we lost the kingdom (righteousness) and because of the fall of man we lost the keys to life. Until we find our way back to the kingdom, the shortage of drinkable water will be a problem. However, if we want to inherit the

Do Not Worry About Water

kingdom that He promised us, He warned us not to worry about where our water was coming from. Instead, "Seek His kingdom and His righteousness and all these things will be added." Yes, having enough drinkable water is a major problem, and in some parts of the world it is a vital problem. It is a matter of life and death.

This problem is so significant that there are people willing to take advantage of a bad situation by creating many false ministries and promising to bring fresh drinking water to some part of the world where drinkable problem is a luxury.

People are dying from the lack of having enough clean water to drink and to carry on with their daily routine that may require the need of water. Remember, 71% of earth is covered with water, but within that percentage 96.5% of the planet's water is found in seas and oceans and only 2.5% of the Earth's water is fresh water, because our Creator always wanted us to utilize the keys that he gave us. The ability to generate machines to produce clean and drinking water for all is essential, and we can't ignore that need. So our Creator gave us the abilities, the capacities, the talents, and the intelligence to design machines to be installed in the water plants in order to generate drinkable water for the world.

So, having clean water to drink could become a major problem when we are not operating the water system with the proper keys. We all have the keys that are needed to make our life easier, we just don't know to which doors they belong. So instead of taking the time to match the keys with the right doors, we instead are opening doors blindly with the hope that we will get lucky one day matching the right doors with the right keys. With God it is not a guessing game. He tells us to seek first and remain in good standing, two important keys. Water is a major problem. Even in most developed countries such as the United States, most people don't trust that their faucet water is good enough to drink, which explains why bottling water is a multi billion dollar industry.

This dilemma is a great business opportunity for some entrepreneurs. After all, they are in business to make money, which is a fact. God warned us that it would be so as a side effect of the fall of man, but He reassured us that we should not panic. We should remain confident that our needs will be met as long as we understand that there is more to life, as long as we apply the Divine Laws and the Principles which were put in place for our own protection which is what Jesus Christ His Son was constantly teaching. "Therefore I tell you, do not worry about your life, what you will eat or drink..." Is that not clear enough for us to understand?

Do you think that God is not aware that the world's population now stands at more than seven plus billion people, many of whom don't currently have access to clean drinking water? Of course He knows all that, because He sees all things and He knows all things. The world's population is increasing which creates the effect of supply/demand on water. The economists named this impact as a disastrous situation that is not going to improve anytime soon. For them it is a time to encourage people to take the risk of investing into the bottled water sales business. Unfortunately, we have it all wrong. Our heavenly Father knew such time would come and He went out of His way to tell us not to fall for it. Instead, remain focused and seek His kingdom and His righteousness and utilize the keys to life. In His kingdom everything is included. Complete access was His original plan for us. We lost it because we did not follow His Divine Laws and His Principles. The promised gift is still ours as long as we seek Him first and be on good standing with His laws and His Principles.

Do Not Worry About Water

What is going on? Why does it seem so difficult to follow such simple instruction? Why is water such an issue all over the world? People are dying because they can't produce food due to a lack of an effective irrigational system. This irrigation problem goes hand in hand with a shortage of water and can only be resolved when a person looks within himself to seek the solution. Remember, God created us in His image, full of gifts, and talents. He created us for a specific purpose, when we don't evaluate ourselves we are unable to find our purpose. Therefore we are withholding solutions to our problems.

I remember when I was growing up in Dufour, in a commune of Miragôane, the farmers had a set time as to when they would have complete access to the river to water their farms. At times the farmers would have a major conflict if another farmer mistakenly changed the set day of watering without their permission. This problem does not only exist in Haiti. Farmers from Africa endure a similar situation. Very recently, in 2003 to be correct, there was a conflict in the Darfur region of Sudan over water. The result of this conflict led to a lack of sufficient food and water and eventually large numbers of migratory farmers had to leave the country.

The misuse and abuse of the purpose of water now created bigger issues for us to manage. Our lack of management also diminishes the quality results of the purpose of water. The fact is we don't understand the use and benefits of the purpose of water. We therefore use it as a dumping ground, which creates issues we are still trying to fix. "The waters' inherent laws have kicked in, no one has to punish us for using the water incorrectly, the water just starts to malfunction and we suffer the consequences."

Triumphing Over Hell On Earth

According to Melissa Belt, when we disregard the Divine Laws and Principles created to protect the purpose of water we end up with problems that we can't comprehend.

A few years ago, when I went back to Haiti, I noticed there were not as many farmers compared to when I was a child. I was told by the few farmers who were still there, that they can no longer cultivate their land because of a lack of water supply. The irrigation system was worse than ever. They had very little rain since most trees had been deforested to build houses and other necessary materials to survive.

Most of the rivers and streams had dried out. In front of my house in Dufour there used to be a little river, which actually necessitated a small a bridge in order to cross. Since my last visit, that river is almost non-existent because of citizens used it as dumping ground. We ignore the purpose of water because we don't even know our purpose. We don't know our identity and the reason why we were created. Haiti is considered lower than a third world country. We have accepted that label and we tend to wear it well. It shows how we accept a mediocre life style and call it living. What is going on? We are following our own agenda. We are not applying the guideline of our Creator. We are not using the keys to life that He had given us as our inherent keys to life "... do not worry about your life, what you will eat or drink..." Why are we worried? Have our worries solved the mystery of the lack of water? Absolutely not, instead we are creating more and more dilemmas.

Most houses in the United States have a water system to purify their water. A water bottle costs more than a soft drink. What we need is to seek His kingdom and His righteousness[26]. Righteousness will be discussed in great detail in a later chapter.

---

[26] Matthew 6:33

Do Not Worry About Water

How can we continue to toil to make ends meet when we are citizens of the kingdom? Our father is the King. He gave us access to everything that He owns. We lost access to the kingdom because we were disobedient to His Divine Laws and His Principles. We lost our dominion, our mandate, our gifts, power to accomplish things on earth according to His will and His purpose for us. He sent His Son Jesus to restore the original plan for us. The access code is simply to "seek first His kingdom and His righteousness and everything will be added into it."[27] This is the best promissory note anyone could wish for. A guarantee to reclaim our access, to regain control of our kingdom, to rediscover our abilities and being able to use our creativity in order to build and design the irrigation system that our nation is waiting for and the water plant that the third world nation is in need of to improve the lives of their children and their children's children. To fully receive the benefit of this promissory note we need to find our purpose.

Purpose

What is purpose? Purpose is the reason why you and I were created. The essence of purpose is to explain the existence and presence of things on earth. Purpose is the answer to all your "whys." Purpose validates the "what." We all have purpose. Each and every human being, big or small, young or old, any ethnicity and race has a purpose. The easy way to understand purpose is to think about your cell phone and ask yourself what is the purpose of this device? How does it validate your daily routine? Now imagine yourself without it? Can you mange your day without it? What would happen if Steve Jobs did not

---

27 Matthew 6:33

understand his purpose to enrich the value of the world of communication?

I was flying Jet Blue to Washington, D.C. and I saw a commercial about "BKask", a system created to transfer money amongst the poorest countries. In that commercial they showcase a young lady who left her country Dahgar, Bengladesh and she was able to take care of her family through that system. She was able to send money to her dad systematically. As a matter of fact, before she left the transfer location, her father already had access to the funds and was able to go to the grocery store and purchase his goods. An underdeveloped country with a powerful device helped the people of the county to better their lives because someone understood his purpose and the needs of the country and made it happen.

The key to a true purpose has to be bigger than just to satisfy your needs, your relatives' needs, and your close friends'.

That concept was not always clear to me. For a while, before I met Trista Sue Kragh, I just wanted to teach, then go home, hoping one day I can retire. I was living in a bubble. I was working hard to instill values and educational purposes into my daughters. I did not understand that while I was teaching my girls the world was waiting to understand the concept of educational purposes as well.

It has been reported that 90% of college freshmen change their major before their senior year. The change is not a bad thing considering the amount of students who returned home to their parents without ever passing one class in college. Why? Because, they have never defined their purpose for their education. Now that I understand my purpose, I have decided to create a plan of action. I wrote a book *Three Steps to Guide Your Children's Educational*

Do Not Worry About Water

Purpose. I decided to contact my local churches to talk to parents about purpose for themselves and for their children.

I realized that my purpose is a mission so I have to reach the students in elementary, middle, and high school. I started to plant the seed of "Purpose" in their lives by creating a "Purposeful, Individualized Educational Plan," PIEP. So I was able to meet with 71 students to help them create a profile about what they think their educational purpose is. I had the support of My College Options, a company that created a detailed educational profile for them based on the degree choice. This profile gave them a list of colleges and universities that offer their degree choice. I plan to take this "Purposeful, Individualized Educational Plan" to colleges and universities hoping I can meet with the freshmen college advisors. I believe if the students are able to define their educational purpose there would be fewer dropouts.

Encouraging others to discover the purpose for their education was always inside of me. It is not because I have a doctoral degree in education. I started encouraging people even before I had my degree in education. I remember the first person I encouraged to pursue her education twenty years ago, is now one of the best innovative teachers for Collier County School District. What I am trying to say is your purpose is inside of you. Schools cannot give it to you but can enhance the seeds that are already inside of you. My migrating to America did not give me my purpose because it was always with me. I had to discover it, which is why I can write about it. My hope is for you to discover your "why" so you can find your "what."

Your "what" is what the world is missing. Trust me, no one can do it better than you. You have the pattern. They can imitate you, but you are the original. The Creator created

Triumphing Over Hell On Earth

each human with a reason and for a reason. He created you with a purpose, and you must seek it.

Do Not Worry About Water

Key Principles:
1. Worry does not make things better, planning does.
2. Be in your season.
3. High standards provide prosperity.
4. Your life does not depend on food alone.
5. How you preoccupied your time is important.
6. Laws and Principles are for your own safety.
7. The order of process is important.

Triumphing Over Hell On Earth

Chapter 3

WHAT SHOULD YOU WEAR

"Therefore I tell you, do not worry about your life, what you will eat or drink; or about your body, what you will wear. Is not life more than food, and the body more than clothes?"[28]

The third lesson taught by the Master Teacher: Do not worry about what you should wear. His essential question was "Can any one of you by worrying add a single hour to your life?"[29]

Our heavenly Father was not just afraid of us being worried over what we would we eat, what we would drink. He was also concerned about us worrying about what we will wear. Yes, clothing, God knew it would be a major issue for us as well. Have you noticed the changes in the fashion industry? Do you see how many designers are competing to get into your closet? Who are you wearing? Who did you wear last year? Last month? Last week? What about yesterday? How many ways can a pair of jeans be designed? The fashion industry is thinking about what our

---

[28] Matthew 6:25
[29] Matthew 6:27

next fashion need would be before we can even think of it? How? They are studying our behavior patterns.

Can you name all the designers? Of course there are designers who are well known such as Michael Kors, Coco Chanel, Alexander Wanj, Raf Simmons, JW Anderson, just to name a few. The point is, fashion is huge not just at a personal level but in the business industry as well. It is a $1.5 trillion dollar industry. The good thing about fashion is, it is also a form of resource for people because it employs millions of people. The bad thing about fashion is it becomes a priority, meaning if we don't have a particular outfit we get dissatisfied. We are charging our purchases to shop for clothes without thinking through the process of how the credit card bills will get paid. We don't really care, as long as we have it in the closet. God did not create us to function in such a manner. This is totally against His original plan of why we were created from the very beginning. We were created to be in control, not to be controlled by clothes. We were created for dominating the fashion industry with our life principles, not the industry dominating our mind process. We are derailing from the original plan and purpose of why we are even here on earth today. We were born to be in charge. We were given "dominion over everything on planet earth" by our Creator, not the other way around.

Genesis 1:26: "Then God said, "Let us make mankind in our image, in our likeness, so that they may rule over the fish in the sea and the birds in the sky, over the livestock and all

What Should You Wear

the wild animals, and over all the creatures that move along the ground."[30]

In the United States some people's closets are big enough to be somebody's house elsewhere. These closets have so many shoes and clothes, sometimes with their tags hanging on them. If items had feelings they would probably feel deprived from not being able to serve their purpose, to be worn. They too were created for a purpose. Hanging inside the closet was not the designer's vision. Yet the owners, not even sure if they can wear them all, nonetheless continue their shopping habits.

Some people are losing their lives over a pair of sneakers. It was reported that a man was killed by a young 16- year-old boy over a pair of limited edition Air Jordan athletic shoes. According to the report, that young boy did not make it to the store on time to purchase his shoes and he was burning of the desire to possess the shoes even if it meant to shoot someone, which is exactly what this young boy did. Killing someone over some shoes!

People are being robbed because they are carrying a designer purse. Some purses cost more than a house. For example, I remember watching one television episode of "Atlanta House Wives " and Porscha, a house wife, was bragging about her new hand bag that she "only paid $80,000" for; also an Hermes Birkin Bag costs $95,750 and

---

[30] Genesis 1:26

people are buying them! You realize that someone could become a first time homebuyer with that same amount of money. As a matter of fact I remember the first home that I purchased in Golden Gate City, Florida was not even that much. Go figure! According to research, more than $250 billion is spent annually on fashion in the United States. New York City and Los Angeles are considered the two largest fashion arenas in the United States.

What are we doing? What about the people who can barely buy a basic pair of pants and shirt to clothe their children for school? Recently, I saw a teacher get nominated for doing an exceptional job, beside her teaching requirement, for taking the time to clothe her students because many of them would come to school dirty. Our Creator warned us not to let our sight misguide us about what clothing items that we may not have in our closet. He warned us not to be confused about all these name brands that are popping up daily. But why? And this is what he said to this matter "Therefore I tell you....about your body, what you will wear. Is not life more than ...the body more than clothes?"

I am sure, if you are like me, when I used to have a religious mindset before I understood the true principles of how things are supposed to function in His realm, you would say, imagine I am walking bare footed, not by choice but because it is my "reality." Some people choose to let their children walk without shoes to build their immune system. No, that is not what I am talking about in this case. I am referring to when your parents look at you in the eye and say

What Should You Wear

to you, "Ok, this is your one pair of shoes for this year. Please take care of them. If you mess them up before the year is over you are on your own." To the point that if it was raining, I knew better than to take them off, because my shoes were more important than my feet. Imagine having to choose protecting your shoes instead of your feet.

I also remember when growing up, I used to have two dresses per year, one for Christmas and the other for Easter. That was it.

The key is we have to see more than our eyes can look. We have to believe that we cannot be told a lie by our Creator because He knows what we need. He knew us even when we were in our mother's belly. "I knew you before I formed you in your mother's womb."[31]

But there is a condition that we need to fulfill. First we need to clearly understand the promise that was made to us by God. Please, don't feel bad if you can't understand His promise, trust me you are not the only one. Many times God had to remind the people of that same promise. This is what He told us in **Matthew 6:28-34**

"And why do you worry about clothes? See how the flowers of the field grow. They do not labor or spin. Yet I tell you that not even Solomon in all his splendor was dressed like one of these. If that is how God clothes the grass of the field, which is here today and tomorrow is thrown into the

---

31 Jeremiah 1:5

fire, will He not much more clothe you—you of little faith? So do not worry, saying…. Or what shall we wear?"[32]

You see, God had to remind us that worry should not be in the equation because it has been determined. He can provide the most expensive name brand line of clothing to us all, but we have to have faith. We have to believe that He is not a storyteller. He is a true God who tells the truth all the time, not sometimes, not most of the time, but all the time.

God said if you are worried about what you should wear, you are not my child, because my children do not worry about such things. He said: "For the pagans run after all these things, and your heavenly Father knows that you need them."[33]

So He is telling us, yes I know you need these items to look good and to protect you as well, because clothing is not just for fashion it protects from weather conditions. For example, when it is cold we have to wear some layers of clothes to keep us warm. When it is hot we have to wear light clothing so we are not burning our skin. God is telling us that He knows all the reasons that we need to have things to wear. "But seek first His kingdom and His righteousness, and all these things will be given to you as well."[34]

---

[32] Matthew 6:28-34
[33] Matthew 6:32
[34] Matthew 6:33

What Should You Wear

This is the condition that we must exemplify in order to have our clothing needs met. God is telling us that it is very simple, you need clothes to wear? Great! But you need to find Him first because He is the source of all that we need. If we seek Him, we will never be without clothes. We will never be in need of what to wear. That is why He tells us if we don't believe Him to take a look at the lilies in the valley. They are looking very fashionable and yet they don't have to do anything, but be in a position to receive.

Why are you worried? Why don't you have enough clothes? Why are you seeking clothes? Why not seek something bigger? Ideas on how to produce the fibers to make the fabric for the clothes, the creative ability to design the latest style, and the vision to build the most prominent clothing line. As a matter of fact, God said, "...do not worry about tomorrow, for tomorrow will worry about itself. Each day has enough trouble of its own."[35] Instead, seek the kingdom for ideas, creativity, vision, and purpose.

Your purpose will predict what you would be. You will find your vision through your purpose. According to Dr. Munroe, "When God gives a vision to someone, He is simply calling forth what He put into that person. This is why you can always determine what you can do by the dream that is within you." You are born where you are because of your purpose. You have the parents who you have because of your purpose. You are the person that you are because of your purpose. You are built the way you are because of your

---

35 Matthew 6: 34

Triumphing Over Hell On Earth

purpose. A friend of mine once told me that she was born to be a massage therapist because of her body structure, and her body strength. She understands that her Creator gave her a purpose. She made it her vision of pursuing a career as a masseuse. She went to school and received the credentials to validate her purpose on earth. Your responsibility is to plant the seed of your vision by believing and acting on it and then nurture that vision by faith, just like my friend did, taking classes and becoming certified.

Faith will help you design the road map that will lead you to your purpose with: The gifts and talents that you have, the dreams that you have, and the thoughts that you constantly have. They don't just happen, just like you, you did not just happen. You were purposefully made. You are the person that you are for a reason and no one else can be you and you cannot be anyone else. You are the perfect you and you don't need to be anyone else. No one can be the perfect you except you, so, for you there is no substitute. The world will not be complete without you being you and fulfilling your purpose.

Therefore, "the greatest tragedy in life is not death, but a life without a purpose" according to Dr. Munroe. God created you with love and He created you with a purpose and a reason in mind. You are the perfect you and only you can fulfill your purpose and we need you to have a complete world around us all. Everyone is necessary. Don't be consumed with the thoughts of not having enough to wear. Instead, let the world be consumed by all your

What Should You Wear

thoughts and vision that you have to transform the fashion industry with your ideas and your creativity.

You may be carrying the vision for the next big fashion trend. According to Dr. Munroe, "Your vision will develop until it is fully grown and bears much fruit in the world." I encourage you to allow the world to benefit and be joyful through your purpose that was given to you by your Creator.

Key Principles

1. Understand the Creator's original plan.
2. Appreciate what you have.
3. Train your eyes to see more than they can look.
4. Success is predictable when you understand the condition.
5. Don't pray for stuff; pray for ideas, purpose, and vision.
6. Your vision is your prayer line.

Chapter 4

SHELTER

Growing up in Haiti, prior to the age of Google search and YouTube, I learned how to use my imagination tremendously. I used to hear people talking about New York so much that I started formulating an idea of what New York may look like. By the way, when I was young, New York was considered America. It was almost like no other states existed.

In Haiti, parents don't have time to answer children's what, where, when, how and why. Therefore, children need to create a way to get their questions answered. I believe I was 9 or 10 years old when I had just moved in with my older brother and his wife from Miragôane to Port-au-Prince. I was so excited to overhear them talking about a friend coming from New York. She was to stay over night because the city she was from was too far and transportation was also an issue. I was so excited of course because I was not supposed to hear that conversation. I couldn't wait to see what our guest from New York would look like.

In my head I was trying to imagine her demeanor, her behavior, and how different she would be from the rest of

Triumphing Over Hell On Earth

us. Unfortunately, I don't remember what she looked like but what I remember is what I did when she went to sleep. As soon as the lady guest and everyone else went to sleep, I was on a mission. I was determined to know what she had in those two big suitcases, so I yielded to my curiosity. I took out every item one by one. I examined each item as if I were a scientist or a crime scene investigator. I was determined to finally have all my questions answered about that "New York" so overtly talked about by adults, not to children, but among themselves.

As a child I heard my parents making plans about New York, and how their lives would be so much better if they could get there one day. They talked about how everything is cold in that place, and you can find money while walking the roads, the "land of honey." Going through the lady's suitcases I began to imagine the smell of New York through the smell of her clothes, I began to visualize how people ate because of the texture of the sugar that she was carrying. I began to imagine how young people my age played because of the toys that she had. If you know how a child can feel at Disney World for the first time. That was I until I couldn't put all the items back into their proper place in the suitcases. I was overwhelmed by all this stuff on the floor. I couldn't remember what went to which suitcase, so I went to bed.

I embarrassed my bother and his wife in front of their guest. They were so ashamed of me. I got the worst beating ever, but I still believe it was worth it because this experience had prepared me for my journey of migrating to America later on. When I was told that I would be moving to America I was excited. In my head I was ready to finally see everything that I had imagined this place to be.

It wasn't so unfortunately. When I left the airport of Miami and entered 48th street North East in Miami, I was so disappointed about America. It couldn't be! Well, it was one room transformed into a bedroom, a kitchen, a bathroom, and a living room for five of us, my mother, my three siblings, and me. My father was living in Immokalee I was told, because of better work opportunities. He would come once in a while. It was a nightmare. I wanted to go back to Haiti. I cried for a whole year. Sometimes it was loud and sometimes it was silent. I would say more silent because I was not sure if my family was feeling as disappointed as I was. So I learned how to keep my emotions to myself.

I could not imagine that people could live in such conditions in America, the land of "milk and honey," the place that parents dreamed of so much. How is this place supposed to change my life when so many of us are sleeping in one bed? I couldn't even have a good night's sleep because of the rats chanting in the ceiling. The worst thing about this house were the weather conditions. When it was hot it was hot, when it was cold it was cold. Regardless of the weather temperature, it was always better to endure the outside temperature because inside that place was always double in degrees compared to the thermometer's indication.

Triumphing Over Hell On Earth

My sheltering condition was so much better in Haiti, I just wanted to go back, but it was not an option for my parents. Later on, my parents decided to make Immokalee our permanent home because both my mother and my father were able to work everyday. The house we moved to was not better than the one in Miami. I began secretly talking to God. I was telling myself this could not be. It has to be better than what I was seeing.

People were happy, my parents were happy, but I wasn't. I am not sure if they noticed my unhappiness. I began planning in my head an exit to this nightmare of living arrangements. I worked in the field of tomatoes and peppers when I was not in school and I would save all my money for my escape plan. One day I heard someone talking about Naples. Just hearing the name of Naples resonated well in my soul. I started thinking and I told myself I needed to see what Naples was all about. I paid a gentleman to drive me to Naples. As soon as I reached Immokalee Road and Hwy. 41, I started feeling at peace with myself. I started admiring the landscaping of the road and I told myself, "This is where you belong."

I needed to seek my own shelter. I found it and I am still living in it. America is the land of opportunity but I learned that I needed to seek it. I needed to look for it. It would not just come at me. I wasn't worried about the situation. I was busy planning and seeking the resources that were available. How far is Naples to Immokalee? Not that far. It takes the desire, which God gave me, and the ability to think which I inherited from my Creator. "God never gave

Shelter

Adam a chair," Dr. Munroe would always say. He gave Adam trees and He told him to become himself. Inside a tree there are many chairs. It was up to Adam to build and design his own chair.

There are great houses in America but simply migrating to America does not guarantee my shelter's stability. I had to desire it and make it happen. I use and apply some keys. I seek and I ask and it was provided. **Matthew 7:7-8** "Ask and it will be given to you; seek and you will find; knock and the door will be opened to you. For everyone who asks receives; the one who seeks finds; and to the one who knocks, the door will be opened."[36]

I wanted a comfortable home. I petitioned my King. He gave me three keys: ask, seek, and knock and I used them. I asked that gentleman to drive me to Naples because I heard him talking about Naples. I let him know that I was seeking a better place to live. He knocked at a few doors for me by asking his friends to help me find an affordable room to rent. According to Dr. Munroe, seeking is "To pursue, study, explore, understand, learn, and consider." He explained that a seeker "must have a desire to know, and possess a passion for their object of their search." I was seeking for an opportunity for a better shelter.

I started utilizing the resources that I had in my possession carefully. I had a job. It was not a dream job but it was giving me the means to accomplish my goal. When I was

---

[36]**Matthew 7: 7-8**

Triumphing Over Hell On Earth

working in the field no one could do it better and faster than me. I was ahead of the line working with the serious migrant workers. To me it wasn't a joke. It was a matter of making it so I could leave one day. The other teenagers would be playing around the field, playing with the farmers' tomatoes or the peppers. Some were told not to return. I knew the field was not my playground. As much as I detested the place I was living, I always kept it clean.

Weekends were the worst time for me, because I would spend the entire weekend cleaning, but my brothers mainly would spend their time making messes. They just didn't get it that God likes order. He is a God of order and if you want to see your way out of any uncontrollable situation, the key is to sort some kind of orderly manners, some kind of organizational system. Until then, it will be very difficult to see the way out. They kept making messes and I kept cleaning.

Later on, I became the prime shelter rescuer for my entire family and family friends who wanted to move to Naples. My first real home in America was 714 11th Street North. I finally had my immaculate landscaping that I imagined America would have for all citizens. This was a prime location, with walking distance to Coastland Mall, walking distance to Naples Beach Club Hotel where my father walked for years to go to work, and walking distance to any luxury life style that Naples had to offer. Finally, I felt like I was living in America. From this point on, no one in my family ever had to go through what I went through on 48th Street North East in Miami. My purpose was to have a decent place to live where I would feel love, joy, and peace because of the

Shelter

presence of the Lord. Many people benefit off the by-product of this vision.

Key Principles

1. Don't live by assumption, live by the truth.
2. Self-evaluation is essential.
3. Your disappointment is the beginning of your success.
4. Planning requires many small steps.
5. Opportunity is always around.
6. When you have questions ask in order to get answer.

Chapter 5

WHAT IS THE KINGDOM OF GOD?

The Kingdom of God: Prerequisite Number One

The word kingdom has been around forever, what does it really mean? Over three thousand years ago Moses recorded the first set of data about the kingdom. Over two thousand years later, after the document of Moses, God commissioned His son Jesus Christ as a master teacher to reteach the original idea of the kingdom that has been mistaught, and misunderstood by all of us due to a religious mindset. The concept of kingdom was also irrelevant to me until I started reading Dr. Munroe's book. He then became my mentor and my spiritual Papa. According to Dr. Munroe, the word kingdom had lost its original intent, because most of the modern world did quite grasp the kingdom concept or idea.

"The concept of kingdom in its original and pure sense has been lost to our modern world. Kingdom as a concept does not exist anymore in the minds of people in Western Civilization, particularly in the past few generations, because all the phototypes either have been destroyed or abandoned. Because there are no kingdoms or remnants of kingdom left in the western world, we live in a generation

Triumphing Over Hell On Earth

where the true meaning of the greatest message ever told cannot be fully understood."

Dr. Munroe later on explained because of that abandoning the world has been impacted tremendously. We can see the effect all over the world. We have nations fighting against nations, we have people of high hierarchy in the government killing civilians without proper justification, and civilians killing people in authority due to confusion and misguidance. You are asking yourself, "What is going on?" The answer is we lost God's original intent for us found in **Genesis 1:26.** Then God said, "Let us make man in our image, according to our likeness; let them have dominion over the fish of the sea, over the birds of the air, and over the cattle, over all the earth and over every creeping thing that creeps on the earth."[37]

Dr. Munroe shaped my understanding of the word kingdom, as he often said "king-dominion." I also understand in order to have a kingdom there must be a king who has dominated his territory based on his values, his principles, and his character in order to create a culture that illustrates the kingdom life style. Culture is very important, because it informs others whom we are without even asking questions.

We talk a lot about culture in the school, because the administrators want visitors to feel and understand the culture the minute they enter the campus. They want the school to display a culture of peace, so parents would feel

---
37 Genesis 1:26

What Is The Kingdom Of God?

at ease knowing that their children will be safe if they become students of that school. They want the school to display a culture of academic excellence. Again, parents want to know that their children will receive the best education if one day they decide to be part of the student body. Parents want a culture of friendliness, respect, and honor and for that reason schools strive very hard to provide that culture within their community.

As you can see, a kingdom has to stand for something and has to represent something, and some prior planning had to be done to have such a result. Most importantly, the king or the person in charge has a responsibility toward his community's well-being.

According to Dr. Munroe, a kingdom is… "the governing influence of a king over his territory, impacting it with his personal will, purpose, and intent, producing a culture, values, morals, and lifestyle that reflect the king's desires and nature for his citizens."

Just as schools strive to let everyone know that they have the culture that symbolizes quality education for all students, God also wanted everyone to know about the culture of His kingdom which is why He sent His only son Jesus Christ to come share that good news with all of us on earth. Jesus Christ was on a special assignment to teach us the prerequisite needed to receive the fruit of the kingdom. God is such a good God. He would never expect something from us without telling us how to get it. God always goes out of His way to give us the guidelines for getting everything that He wants us to have in order to reflect His goodness and His glory.

For that matter, our Father, our King is obligated toward meeting our needs. He has a responsibility toward us which is why He made clear to us that in His kingdom, His community, His citizens should not have to worry. His community's needs shall be met on time as long as we seek first His kingdom and next His righteousness. Then everything should be fine with us. He tells us if we realize that we don't have the kingdom that we should ask for it. Just like parents. Before choosing a school for their children they go online and conduct research about the culture of the school of choice because they are looking for or seeking a particular culture for their children.

You may be wondering how do I search or ask for this kingdom? **Matthew 6:8-10** tells us how and warns us not to be like other people, meaning people who are not searching and seeking the right culture.

"Do not be like them, for your Father knows what you need before you ask Him. "This, then, is how you should pray: "Our Father in heaven, hallowed be your name, your kingdom come, your will be done, on earth as it is in heaven."[38] God also explains to us that in His kingdom some things are done differently. His citizens have a certain lifestyle, there is a code of conduct that must be followed by His citizens.

---

38 Matthew 6:8-10

What Is The Kingdom Of God?

There is an established culture in place for us to follow because we reflect His glory. Jesus Christ explained it to us in **Matthew 6:34** "so do not worry, saying, 'What shall we eat?' or 'What shall we drink?' or 'What shall we wear?' For the pagans run after all these things, and your heavenly Father knows that you need them." Basically He is telling us in His kingdom the culture is a worry free-zone. There is plenty of food, all kinds even if you want gluten-free. There is clean water, and top of the line designers waiting to tailor your garments, a worry-free culture.

Once parents find the school that represents the culture that will meet the academic needs of their children, the next step is to register them. However, there is a list of items they must have in order to qualify their children to attend the school.

Now here is a key point: the children are not automatically qualified to attend the school just because the parents did their research and like the results. There is a registration process to complete before one can attend a school. For example, parents have to supply a proof of address, the child's proof of age, and a health record just to name a few items of prerequisite.

God also has a prerequisite for us in order to make ourselves qualify to receive the goodness that His kingdom provides. **Matthew 6:33** 1) Seek first His kingdom and 2) His righteousness, and all these things will be given to you as well.[39] Just like parents comparing schools before making a decision, we too can make a comparison if we have a religious mindset. We are not the only ones who have ever thought about comparing God's kingdom with other things, in previous times, other people had the same religious mindset.

Luke 13:20-21 "Again he asked, 'What shall I compare the kingdom of God to? It is like yeast that a woman took and mixed into a large amount of flour until it worked all through the dough."

Indeed the kingdom of God is contagious. Once you have it you must spread its goodness to others. As Dr. Munroe would say, "Pass it on." The kingdom of God is love, peace, and joy; the three ingredients that we are all seeking with the hope that our life will be better. The truth is, our life is better when we are in the kingdom of God, and when we understand and apply the kingdom concept. The kingdom comes with advantages and benefits. We tend to forget who we are. That is why God sent His Son Jesus Christ to remind us about the care package that has already been put aside for us. We have full guarantee that it is not necessary to worry about some basic life necessities such as food, water, and shelter. **Matthew 6:27** Can any one of you by worrying add a single hour to your life"[40] and, "Therefore do not worry about tomorrow, for tomorrow will worry about itself. Each day has enough trouble of its own."[41]

---

39 Matthew 6:33
40 Matthew 6: 27
41 Matthew 6: 34

What Is The Kingdom Of God?

As you can see worry is not the way to operate in the kingdom of God. Worry only produces stress, which causes sickness. The best way is to rely mainly on the Creator's promises, because He will always fulfill our needs.

Key Principles

1. Dislocation is temporary.
2. Culture displays values, principles, and character.
3. What does your culture say about you.
4. Stand for something important.
5. Know your life mission, because we all have one.
6. Your Creator has a responsibility toward your needs.
7. You have to make yourself qualify.
8. Be in position to receive.

Chapter 6

WHAT IS GOD'S RIGHTEOUNESS

Righteousness: Prerequisite Number Two

The second prerequisite was mandated and reintroduced and retaught by Jesus Christ because that was His purpose in coming to earth. God was determined and is still determined that we regain this concept of kingdom, His original plan for us since the very beginning as stated in **Genesis 1:26** "He made in His image, based on His likeness, and He gave us dominion over the fish of the sea, over the birds of the air, and over the cattle, and over every creeping thing that creeps on the earth."[42]

God never told us to have dominion over people, He never told us to have dominion over other nations, and He never told us to have dominion over people who may be less powerful than we are. Somehow we misunderstood His mandate, and His purpose and we began to dominate the wrong things, because it is within us to be in control. When God created us, He built us with the ability and the capacity to dominate, not be dominated by one another and this is where the chaos began. We feel out of place or out of

---

[42] Genesis 1: 26

Triumphing Over Hell On Earth

order when we are told what to do because it is within us not to receive orders but to give orders.

What we don't understand is to whom should we manifest our dominion power? God made it clear to us: "fish of the sea, birds in the air, over the cattle, over all the earth and over every creeping thing that creeps on the earth." God understood that we misunderstood His original plan. Therefore we became out of order. We became out of alignment, we are not under His authority, and we begin to worry about what we will eat, what we will drink, what we will wear, and where we will stay while He had created everything that we would need. Now let's think about it. There is no way God would bring us on earth and not provide the supplies to meet our basic needs, impossible. We missed it! So God had to do it again. He sent us a Master Teacher to reteach us the concept because we failed the test more than once.

From that time on Jesus began to preach, "Repent, for the kingdom of heaven is near"[43]**Matthew 5:3.**

It was important for Him to reteach this concept because we have to meet the standard of the two prerequisites established by God in order for us to receive His promise; first seek His kingdom, second be in righteousness.

Again, I have to use the definition of Dr. Munroe for righteousness. He explains that the word righteousness is

---

[43] Matthew 5:3

What Is God's Righteousness?

"from discipline of law, not religion, and implies right positioning."

According to Dr. Munroe, when we are in righteousness, we are "in alignment with authority, we are standing with authority, we have the right fellowship with authority, we are in right relationship with authority, we are in legal or lawful alignment, and we are in correct standing with the law or the regulations or principles of and to fulfill the requirements of authority."

I came to the realization that if we are not under His authority, if we are not following His standard to execute our ideas, and we don't align our to-do list with His, we are living a nightmare. We become oppressed, depressed, suicidal, low-esteemed, and we are discouraged because we are not in alignment. We are running around without a plan, when a plan was crafted, designed, and put in place for us to model. Jesus said, "first seek His kingdom, second His righteousness, and all things will be given to you as well"[44] **Matthew 6:33.**

Everything will be given to you, not something, but everything. Ask yourself these questions. What are you lacking? And Why? Why don't you have everything that you need? Why are you always in need of something? Why can't your needs be met on time? Why don't you have enough money to pay for your rent? Why are you working so hard to pay bills? Why are you in debt? Are you seeking His

---
[44] Matthew 6:33

kingdom? Are you in His righteousness? Are you dominating the earth or the earth dominating you?

How do you get back on track? How do you follow the plan that was crafted and designed for you to model?

Think and meditate about these simple questions and assess your environment.

- What can you do differently to make it right?
- How do you get back in the game?

You are a meaningful player. The team needs you to win. Your country needs your ideas to get to the next level. Your generation needs you to get ahead. We need you to diminish poverty, and to provide clean water to people who are dying because of lack of basic human needs. How do we get back? Seek first His kingdom and His righteousness.

It is extremely important for us to remain righteous. According to Dr. Munroe, the essence of being righteous "is the maintenance of the rightly aligned relationship with a governing authority so as to qualify for the right to receive governmental privileges." The right to receive kingdom benefits, this has been arranged. I hope you understand why Jesus' mandate was so important and why Jesus only taught one lesson, "the kingdom and the need to be righteous so that you can receive all the benefits that come with it." This promissory note includes all basic human needs such as food, water, clothing, and shelters.

When I first rediscovered the kingdom and its benefits I wanted to share this good news with all my friends and my

What Is God's Righteousness?

relatives. The first person I approached was my best friend and my pastor. I was so excited and I knew she would be excited as well. She has been my Christian role model for years. I learned everything I know about Jesus through her ministry. Unfortunately, she has not been able to understand the kingdom and its benefit to the degree that I understand it, but I remain confident that she will one day. Jesus' mission on earth was to reestablish His Father's mandate for mankind: "the kingdom of God and the righteousness of God. Kingdom refers to the government influence of heaven on earth and righteousness refers to right alignment and positioning with the government authority.

It is simple with some complexity for some people, but if you follow the laws and you do what you are supposed to do then the government has a responsibility toward your needs. When I had the religious mindset, I couldn't relate to this statement. I thought I had to beg all the time, I did not know there were guidelines, Divine Laws, and Principles to follow. If I position myself under my King's authority He is obligated to meet my needs.

Wow! What a process. This is easy. It was so clear to me I expected everyone to understand it as well. My best friend who pastors a church at times would get into financial difficulty to meet the church's obligation and I would share with her how it would work if her members understood the benefit of having the right alignment, the right positioning with their authority. Jesus used many parables when He was teaching the kingdom because He wanted the people to understand the significance of having the right keys. This is

Triumphing Over Hell On Earth

how He did it according to **Matthew 13:31-32** He told them another parable: "The kingdom of heaven is like a mustard seed, which a man took and planted in his field. Though it is the smallest of all seeds, yet when it grows, it is the largest of garden plants and becomes a tree, so that the birds come and perch in its branches."[45]

I kept encouraging my friend to first seek His kingdom and His righteousness[46] for herself then pass it on to her members then she wouldn't have to toil so much.

It is a work in progress for me to truly have a rightly aligned relationship with my government authority who is my King, but my goal is to remain under such authority because as long as I do my part I am fully covered.

---

45 Matthew 13: 31-32
46 Matthew 6: 33

Key Principles:

1. Righteousness is being in good standing with authority.
2. Your dominion is not over other people, but over your gift.
3. Repentance is acknowledging that you were wrong.
4. Born again is a mental transformation.
5. When you are under authority you have complete access.
6. You are a meaningful team player.
7. You have a responsibility toward your government, and your government has a responsibility toward you.

Triumphing Over Hell On Earth

Chapter 7

HOW TO ENTER THE KINGDOM OF GOD

Isaiah 48:17-18 "This is what Jehovah says, your Redeemer, the Holy One of Israel: "I, Jehovah, am your God, The One teaching you to benefit yourself, The One guiding you in the way you should walk. If only you would pay attention to my commandments! Then your peace would become just like a river. And your righteousness like the waves of the sea."[47]

We finally understand that there is more to life than what we will eat, what we will drink, what we will wear, and where we will stay. We understand life has more to offer than losing our mind over simple basic human needs. How do we get there? What is the way? And if you have a religious mindset like I used to, the next question should be "if it is so simple, why haven't you found the solution to hunger? Why is having sufficient drinkable water still a luxury for many parts of the world?" I validate your questions and I understand your thinking process because I was once there until I understood the kingdom process. We understand that Jesus said, "Seek first the kingdom of God." But what does it mean

---

47 Isaiah 48: 17-18

Triumphing Over Hell On Earth

to you? Why is it necessary? How can we accomplish this command?

This process requires two things. First you must repent and second you must believe and be baptized.

I will take the time and explain each phase so we can understand the kingdom process that our Master Teacher Jesus Christ was teaching. It is told that Jesus only taught one lesson "Repent, for the kingdom of heaven is near"[48] **Matthew 5:3.** Repent is a transformation of the mind. It is critical for us to repent because we "all have sinned and fall short of the glory of God"[49]. To repent means we have to change our "normal way" of thinking, because it is against God's will. We have an obligation to reflect our King's character, because we represent Him in our system, our work place, our community, and in our environment.

Remember, a kingdom is "The governing influence of a king over his territory, impacting it with his personal will, purpose, and intent, producing a culture, values, morals, and lifestyles that reflect the king's desires and nature for his citizens," according to Dr. Munroe.

Jesus said, "If you want to enter into life, keep the commandments."[50] That means reflect the culture of the king in your behavior, reflect His character in your language, and display His values by your choices.

---

48 Matthew 5:3
49 Romans 3:23
50 Matthew 19:17

How To Enter The Kingdom Of God

This transformation is a process that troubles many people because from the minute we are born our mind begins to collect and store data and information whether good or bad. We don't differentiate. We just collect and store. By the time we reach puberty, our minds have been conditioned by our surroundings, our environment, our society, our culture, our families, our friends, and our social media friends. Yet, Jesus tells us that we have to transform that mindset to a different mindset in order to enter the kingdom of God.

According to Jesus we need to think like a child, without limitation, believe everything is possible. We have to emulate the kingdom definition mentioned above. As children, we believe everything our parents tell us. A child-minded person is not yet poisoned with negativity and limitation. Jesus Christ taught about repentance. It is also told that some miracles were happening during His teaching not to convince the people about the kingdom, but because in the kingdom good things happen.

In the kingdom there is no sickness, people are fed on time, fresh water is available, people are not worried about shelter. The miracles were not to attract the people although it seems like they were more interested in the miraculous signs rather than the teaching. Miracles were happening because it was the culture. People were questioning themselves about who Jesus was and how to become like him. According to **John 3: 1-3,** "Now there was a Pharisee, a man named Nicodemus who was a member of the Jewish ruling council. He came to Jesus at night and said, "Rabbi, we know that you are a teacher who has come from God. For no one could perform the signs you are doing if God were not with him." Jesus replied, "Very truly I tell you, no one can see the kingdom of God unless they are born again."[51]

Jesus is telling us that we have to think like a child. We have to repent. In this context, repent means we have to have a new way of thinking. We have to "deprogram" our thought process; we have to delete all these limitations and the negativity we have stored in our mind. We have to clear out all the lies that our society has told us about ourselves. And now we have to reprogram our minds with the kingdom principles, the values, the character, and the culture in order to receive the keys to life. Jesus said the only way to get this process done is to think like a child and believe like a child.

Belief is the second phase of the process to enter the kingdom of God. Now belief is to allow yourself to embrace and to accept things that are out of your realm. To believe is the capacity to dream big, so big that your friends may think that you are out of your mind! That is belief. When we begin to believe, we begin to connect with our King and we begin to accept His influence in our lives. We begin to let our territory be impacted by His territory. We begin to let His will be our will. We begin to understand His purpose for our lives purpose and we begin to reproduce His culture, His values within our daily activities.

---

[51] John 3: 1-3

How To Enter The Kingdom Of God

We have to believe that Our heavenly Father is able to do all things without limitation, so when we find ourselves in the midst of poverty we have to believe that we can change our situation by believing and by exercising our faith that if we ask we will receive. **Hebrew 11:1,** "Now faith is confidence in what we hope for and assurance about what we do not see." We have not yet seen how we are going to solve the hunger problem, but we have faith that we will solve it because we were created in God's image with creativity and ability to solve problems. All we have to do is to believe in ourselves that we can do it. We have to evaluate our resources and evaluate our capacity to assess the needs and make a plan of action according to His will. **John 16:4,** "How can someone be born when they are old?" Nicodemus asked. "Surely they cannot enter a second time into their mother's womb to be born!"[52] We can be born again by changing our ways to His ways, and recognizing that we are sinners, but we have been promised a second chance to make it better; a second chance to find our identity and recognize that we were created with purpose, with gifts, with talents, and we were assigned a specific task on earth to accomplish.

Assess the problem in your community and ask yourself, "How can I solve this problem?" We can no longer allow our circumstance to define us. We have to seek opportunities because they are everywhere. Mathias Pierre said in his book, <u>*The Power of a Dream,*</u> "Opportunities are sometimes

---

[52] John 16: 4

hiding in plain sight, and people need to learn how to recognize and take advantage of them when they are available." The only way you can recognize opportunity is by "seeing more than your eyes can look," is by changing your mind and making a determination to make a difference, also by believing that you can do it regardless of what your environment is telling you. Regardless of the color of your skin, regardless if you speak a different language, regardless if you are from a different country, your gift is good enough for the high food demands, your gift is critical to the irrigation system, and your creativity is essential to take on the fashion industry all over the world, not just in New York, Los Angeles, London and Paris. Jesus Christ was sent to earth with one mission: to teach us how to seek the kingdom and its righteousness through the application of repentance and belief by increasing our faith in order to receive the Holy Spirit through baptism.

Baptism in the Holy Spirit

The ability to communicate with one another is very critical. There are many forms of communication. We can communicate face-to-face. We can communicate in writing. We can communicate over the phone. Presently, we have virtual communication via email, Facebook, Twitter, Instagram and many more. The point is we must communicate to maintain a relationship, to keep up with the relationship and to understand what is going on around us. This is practically the same if we want to assess the situation between God and us. We have to communicate with Him. If we want to maintain the relationship we have with Him we must therefore communicate with Him.

How To Enter The Kingdom Of God

The Holy Spirit helps us to communicate with God. We all have access to the Holy Spirit but not all of us know how to access it. Not all of us use it to improve the relationship that we have with God. According to Dr. Munroe the Holy Spirit is "A distinct being who grants us knowledge and power when we have a relationship with the King and when we yield to the will of the kingdom." Dr. Myles referred to the Holy Spirit as a person that we receive in the new birth process.

How to Receive the Holy Spirit?

There is a process to receive the Holy Spirit. I hope you realize that there is always a process with God. If you are unsure of where to begin with your life, start by seeking the process. God is a God of order. He always lays out the plan with the steps to accomplish the plan.

The process to receive the Holy Spirit begins with repentance. We must understand that our minds have to change. We have to transform our mindset just like a child. We have to change the way we have been living and choose the desire to live our lives by the standards of the Heavenly kingdom. Second, we have to start applying the newly learned principles in our lives to reflect that new mindset: culture, values, character, and morals. Then we have to be baptized to receive the power of the Holy Spirit.

Baptism is more than the water or just the action of being baptized. It has to do with that mind transformation you choose to undergo in order to be in good standing with your

Triumphing Over Hell On Earth

King. It is the lifestyle transformation that reflects the King's moral values and standards. Jesus Christ, the Master Teacher was 30 years old when He was baptized by His cousin John. Jesus understood the process of being in good standing with His Father so He told John "Let it be so now; it is proper for us to do this to fulfill all righteousness." As soon as Jesus was baptized, He went up out of the water. At that moment heaven was opened, and He saw the Spirit of God descending like a dove and lighting on Him. And a voice from heaven said. "This is my son, whom I love; with Him I am pleased." [53] Jesus demonstrated how He was in right standing with His father in order to accomplish His task.

When I was going through the motion in the religious world that concept was totally unclear to me. Once I understood the process and the benefit of receiving the Holy Spirit I contacted Kragh, my spiritual mentor, and asked her to baptize me in order to position myself in good standing with my King. I had to recognize that I am a sinner and I wanted to change that. What should I do? Peter said, "Repent, and let every one of you be baptized in the name of Jesus Christ for the remission of sins; and you shall receive the gift of the Holy Spirit."[54] So I did under the authority of Kragh who had introduced me to the kingdom and taught me the meaning of living a kingdom lifestyle. My life has changed forever. This is a very important process to understand and to accomplish because the Holy Spirit is what we lost when man fell. We lost the kingdom, our dominion.

---

53 Matthew 3: 15-16
54 Acts 2:38

How To Enter The Kingdom Of God

According to the Bible, the kingdom of God is: Love, Peace, Joy in the Holy Spirit. When you find yourself going with the motion and asking "What is next?" or "Is that all?" let me remind you that void is what you lost, the Kingdom. Until you find it, just like I had to find it, you will have many sleepless nights, and many unanswered questions because you are not looking in the right place. "Seek first His kingdom and His righteousness and everything else will be added into it."[55] The kingdom of God is the authority over the earth. It is the dominion over the earth. Baptism prepares us for earth, to restore our dominion in order to make earth a replica of heaven "...whatever you bound on earth will be bound in heaven, and whatever you lose on earth will be lost in heaven." **Matthew 16:19**

Baptism is a covenant we make with our God and His Son Jesus Christ. It symbolizes our understanding that we have broken His law and principles and we are desperately in need of being forgiven of our mismanaging of our resources.

It is a contract that signifies our commitment to obey His law and to reflect His culture.

Now we have the tools needed to help us seek His kingdom and His righteousness. We finally have the process required to make ourselves qualify to receive all the benefits that the kingdom promises to give us if we are in good

---

[55] Matthew 6:33

Triumphing Over Hell On Earth

standing. We also understand that we are made in God's image. That gives us the same ability to do even greater things than He did. "Very truly I tell you, whoever believes in me will do the works I have been doing, and they will do even greater things than these..."[56] It is a matter to evaluate ourselves, our skills, our abilities, our creativities in order to assess the problems that our third world nations are going through such as the agricultural skills needed to cultivate the lands in order to provide enough food to feed seven plus billion people, to solve the irrigation problem in order to diminish the need for clean water, and architects to build affordable housing.

This is necessary in order to understand what to learn and in order to come up with innovative ideas to design water pumps or water chemical plants for people who are living in underdeveloped countries. We must accept that we have a responsibility toward ourselves because God gives us the ability to manage the kingdom resources, which are available to us all the time, and if we neglect that task our Father will not be pleased with us.

We don't want to be like that servant who hid his trusted gold instead of investing it to make a profit, as did his friends. Jesus had a name for such behavior. He called it "wicked and lazy." Our creator wants us to be productive, and use our resources to make Him proud, we have His image. **Matthew 25: 24-26,** "Then the man who had received one bag of gold came. 'Master,' he said, 'I knew that you are a

---

[56] John 14:12

How To Enter The Kingdom Of God

hard man, harvesting where you have not sown and gathering where you have not scattered seed. So I was afraid and went out and hid your gold in the ground. See, here is what belongs to you.' "His master replied, 'You wicked, lazy servant! So you knew that I harvest where I have not sown and gather where I have not scattered seed?"[57]

As a matter of fact if we don't use our resources properly He will take them away from us and give them to other people who can manage them. You have a "responsibility toward your ability." You have the resources you need to put them to use. This is what He did to that servant who could not think hard enough to use his potential. This is how **Matthew 25:28-29** explains it: "So take the bag of gold from him and give it to the one who has ten bags. For whoever has will be given more, and they will have abundance. Whoever does not have, even what they have will be taken from them."[58] Yes he will take it away if you can't manage it properly."

When Jesus said in **Matthew 6: 25**, "Therefore I tell you, do not worry about your life, what you will eat or drink; or about your body, what you will wear. Is not life more than food, and the body more than clothes?"[59] I can only imply that He wants us to see the bigger picture, not just seeking basic human needs because we are the tools to provide these things. We have the tools to produce these things. We just

---

[57] Matthew 25: 24-26
[58] Matthew 25:28-29
[59] Matthew 6: 25

Triumphing Over Hell On Earth

have to accept the fact of where we may be at the present moment and to assess the opportunities that are hiding within the disaster that we are facing.

God places you where He needs you to be because you have a task to accomplish. But you have to believe and have faith because you are stronger than you may think you are. You have skills that are waiting to be discovered, you have talents that are waiting to be polished, and you have accomplishments that need to be uncovered.

Why are you waiting? Today is your day. Get up and take the steps that you are so afraid of, the steps that you cannot see because you are looking with your eyes. You need to use your heart so you can hear the Holy Spirit guiding your vision to improve the world. You need more than just the basic needs as Jesus stated, "Man shall not live by bread alone, but by every word that proceeds from the mouth of God." [60] We matter, the world matters, your purpose matters, and your vision matters, so let's make it happen.

---

[60] Matthew 4:4

Key Principles:

1. Life is more than just searching for basic human needs.
2. Transformation is a change of mind.
3. A child like mind is needed to be transformed.
4. Faith is the currency that is used in the kingdom government.
5. Believe is the ability to dream big.
6. Poverty could be a mindset.
7. Opportunities are hiding in plain sight.
8. The Holy Spirit is a communication device between you and your Creator.

Triumphing Over Hell On Earth

Chapter 8

HOW TO DESCRIBE THE KINGDOM OF GOD
Cross References

Matthew 13:24
Jesus told them another parable: "The kingdom of heaven is like a man who sowed good seed in his field."

Matthew 13:31
He told them another parable: "The kingdom of heaven is like a mustard seed, which a man took and planted in his field.

Matthew 13:32
Though it is the smallest of all seeds, yet when it grows, it is the largest of garden plants and becomes a tree, so that the birds come and perch in its branches."

Mark 4:30
Again he said, "What shall we say the kingdom of God is like, or what parable shall we use to describe it?

Luke 13:20
Again he asked, "What shall I compare the kingdom of God to?

Triumphing Over Hell On Earth

Luke 13:22
He told them still another parable: "The kingdom of heaven is like yeast that a woman took and mixed into about sixty pounds of flour until it worked all through the dough."

Luke 13-44-45
"The kingdom of heaven is like a treasure hidden in the field, which a man found and hid again; and from joy over it he goes and sells all that he has and buys that field. 45"Again, the kingdom of heaven is like a merchant seeking fine pearls,..."

Chapter 9

SELF-DISCOVERY

"When problems meet the gift, wealth is the result."
Dr. Myles Munroe

Self-discovery is very critical if problems are to be solved. Most of the time we have the solutions for many incidents that are occurring around us but due to a lack of self-assessment we miss the opportunity to solve them. Self-discovery is a process. It requires you to answer some simple questions to help you evaluate your self-worth. This process can also help uncover your hidden gifts, talents, and the ultimate purpose for your creation.

We were told that basic human needs such as food, water, clothing, and shelter should not be a concern. Seeking the Kingdom and his righteousness is how we should prioritize our search. The Kingdom was prepared for us since the creation of the world, yet in order to profit from its benefit we need to know our position. We need to know who we are. We need to understand that we were created with specific gifts and talents because there is a special task awaiting our creativity.

Triumphing Over Hell On Earth

Due to life circumstances we tend to over look or minimize our natural abilities. Again, because it is "natural," we ignore its significance. Instead, we chase the wrong thing. We were taught the *dos* and the *don'ts* by a Master Teacher, the best who ever existed. First, don't worry about food. Second, don't worry about water. Last, don't worry about clothing and shelter, but do seek first the kingdom and his righteousness. If you seek them first, you will also find and understand your purpose, the ultimate reason you were created. It requires some thinking process, which is one of the most complex things to accomplish, yet necessary to develop self-growth. Thinking is a difficult function because it requires self-responsibility, self-control, and self-discipline in order to reach the standards that your Creator has for you. It is easier to maneuver daily routines that do not require thinking, although the thought of not thinking is an action where thinking is taking place, subconsciously, because you chose not to think. It may not be productive thinking, nonetheless it is thinking.

There are some guidelines to follow during the self-discovering stage. The first step is to answer the eleven questions that follow. Also, I encourage you to write a reflection about what you discover about yourself. This is an opportunity to have a self-talk. You can begin the thinking process with the following two questions: 1. How can I change my present situation? 2. How can I transform it into a successful opportunity? You can change your present situation by the awareness of your existence and why. You can also transform it into a successful opportunity by identifying the essential *reason* you were created. You may

Self Discovery

be wondering, "What is that essential reason?" The essential reason is to identify and define your purpose. Your purpose carries all the secret codes you need to become yourself. It carries all the tools you need to begin the blue print of your destiny. Once you determine that purpose, you should stick to it, seek a plan to develop it, and protect it with Divine laws and principles. The first step is to answer these twelve self-discovering questions:

1. What is My Deepest Desire? Not what I have a general or passing "interest" in, but rather a deep yearning or aspiration to do.
2. What Am I Truly Passionate About? What do I really care about? What gifts and abilities do I especially enjoy using?
3. What Makes Me Angry? Not destructive anger which is selfishly motivated, but constructive anger that is based on compassion for others and a desire for people to be treated right; anger that is grieved by injustices and that leads to positive action to remedy problems.
4. What Ideas Are Persistent In My Heart, Mind, and Thoughts? What recurring dreams do I have for my life? What idea(s) never leaves me?
5. What Do I Constantly Imagine Myself Doing? What do I dream about becoming? What gifts or skills would I use and develop in order to become this?
6. What Do I Want to Do for Humanity? What kind of impact would I like to have on my community? What do I want to pass along to the next generation? What would I like to be remembered for?

Triumphing Over Hell On Earth

7. What Brings Me the Greatest Fulfillment? What three endeavors or achievements have given me the greatest satisfaction and fulfillment in life so far, and why? What motivates and gratifies me the most, and how can I incorporate it into my life as my vocation or life focus?
8. What Could I Do Forever Even If There Were No Monetary Compensation? From what activities am I currently receiving satisfaction that I'm not being paid for? What am I so dedicated to that I would continue to do it even if I stopped receiving money for it? What would I do for no compensation?
9. What Would I Rather Be Doing? What do I wish I were doing when I am doing other things? What makes me feel most at home when I am doing it?
10. What Would I Do If I Knew I Could Not Fail? What endeavor, enterprise, creative work, project, or plan would I engage in if it were risk-free? If money were no object? If I didn't worry that I had the wrong background, the wrong looks, the wrong job experiences, or the wrong anything else?
11. What is the Most Important Thing I could Do With My Life? Above all other things, what is the most significant thing I could do with my life? What do I want to occur in my life? How do I want to live my life based on my values and beliefs?
12. What Endeavor or Activity Would Best Connect Me to My Creator? What draws me closest to God?

The answers to these questions are the beginning blueprint of your transformational plan for your purpose. At

Self Discovery

this point you can begin the writing process of the reflection of your purpose. Remember, "When problems meet the gift, wealth is the result," Dr. Munroe. The world is full of problems and needs and you carry the solutions, so get busy. There are blank pages provided at the end of this chapter for that purpose. You can write how well you imagine the process of this change will be for the next year, two years or four years or more. You can create the ideal setting since you have discovered the purpose. The time has arrived to begin seeing more than what your eyes can look. It is time to start thinking about the steps you will take to attend your purpose. This step requires a planning process.

Key Principles

1. Self-discovery is a process.
2. This process can help you uncover your hidden talents and gifts.
3. Not thinking is thinking.
4. Your purpose carries all the secret codes you need to become yourself.
5. Planning makes life easier.

Chapter 10

PLANNING

"Failing to Plan is Planning to Fail."
"The answer is right inside of us. It's our attitudes that make the difference."
Dr. Myles Munroe

Planning is the last thing people think about, yet it is extremely important in order to monitor the progress of any purposeful decision. The planning phase involves the thinking process required to make your purpose a reality, the vision that you have in your head. Vision is the solution to the problems you have been trying to avoid for so long. Now you can begin the planning process on how you will develop a system to diminish the scarcity of basic human needs: water, food, water, and shelter.

Planning gives meaning to your vision. It will help you to stay organized. With proper planning, you can achieve your purpose. Establishing and learning how to prioritize through planning is the key component to drive your transformational journey successfully. Any other elements that do not belong to the purpose of your plan must be put aside or completely eliminated regardless of whether or not it is a good plan. Unless it aligns with your purpose it must be rejected. A good plan can hinder the purpose when it does not fit part of your journey.

I remember when I went back to college while raising two girls as a single mother. I had to do a lot of planning. I had to plan my schedule around their schedules so I could be around to take care of them, most importantly to protect them. I had to plan my work schedule. I couldn't stop working and just go to school. I had to continue running my beauty salon and taking classes. As you can see, I had to do major planning in order to effectively utilize the 24 hours I had available to me.

I did it. I was able to graduate *Summa Cum Laude* and on time. I managed to keep my daughters very busy in school. They played clarinet in the band, they ran cross county and track and field, they were on the swim team, they made it to the dance team, they played tennis, they did theater in school and within the community, just to name a few activities. As you can see I did not deprive my girls the opportunity to do extracurricular activities while I was trying to improve my skills. I learned that planning was the only way I could prioritize my life and their lives. A well thought plan was the only effective force of defense that was able to securely guide my transitional journey. It can also help your journey. A well-balanced plan will help you learn how to prioritize your time and how to remain focused in order to achieve your purpose successfully. A plan is a very important document to have since we change our minds all the time.

Planning

We need to learn how to make a contract (pledge) with ourselves.

We make contracts in every aspect in our lives. We sign contracts when we purchase a car, when we take classes, when we get a credit card, and when we rent a house. We pledge to obey other people's demands or standards. Do you ever wonder why we have such a hard time following through or making good with these "contracts?" Because we don't plan, we just do. According to Dr. Munroe when you don't have a plan for your life "you will be confused, disoriented, misguided, and frustrated." If you want to make progress you must have a plan. The plan will help you understand how to organize your time during the day. It will help you to define and set standards for your purpose. The standard will not be based on just going with the flow; rather it will be about how well you can achieve your purpose based on your potentials, your abilities, your gifts, and your talents. God says, "You make the plan and I will give you the answer to how it will be accomplished."

A plan will set you apart from mediocrity to superiority. The greatest impact of your transformational journey is not having a clear plan structured enough to protect your purpose. Your purpose is important. Therefore, you have to protect it with Divine laws and principles. According to Dr. Munroe "God didn't want success in life to be haphazard but predictable. So He built in life laws & principles. Operate life in principles, not effort." The right principles are essential for you to guide your purpose. You have to nurture it.

Triumphing Over Hell On Earth

You need to both nurture and mentor your plan. It is critically important for you to understand the purpose of your journey so you can be successful. Your purpose can be impacted by the many choices and options are available. You must remain focused to make it a reality and to achieve success. Kragh stated in her book *Figure it Out* that:

"God did not create life to be complicated or a mystery. He created everything in life to succeed. That is the reason for us having His principles to guide us in life; we are guaranteed success. These principles are also known as the Laws of God, keys or principles. God's Laws are built into creation."

It is predictable if we can achieve our purpose and make it a vision based on the choices we make. It is predictable if we can have all our basic needs met based on decisions we make. What you think, what you see, what your friends think and see are not what God sees. He sees potential, purpose, vision, and world changers. A seed of a mango tree carries the fruits (more mangoes) which means you are the solution to world hunger, you are the solution to clean water, you are the solution for clothing and shelter for third world nations and people with third world mentality.

How do you make the right choice regarding your purpose? Is there a problem in particular that gets you out of bed, or keeps you up all night? What issues propel your thought process each day? What individual or world problem is consuming your thoughts? These questions can be overwhelming for you. These are difficult questions for

Planning

you to answer, but seeking the answers is the vehicle to navigating your journey successfully. Mathias Pierre, Presidential candidate of Haiti for 2016, just like the other candidates, is consumed with the thought that Haitian children don't have equal educational access, don't have enough food to eat, and most Haitians don't have access to equal rights as it is in other countries. Most people who know Mathias Pierre can't understand why a self-made Haitian millionaire would be stressing about other Haitian people's problems. His answer would simply be, "A change needs to come forth for my Haitian people." Candidate Mathias Pierre explains that he is no different than those children, he chose to have a plan for his life and he says:

"The person I am today is a product of the trials and the adversity that molded me. I grew up in the midst of the abject poverty that is prevalent in many parts of Haiti. I know what it means to be hungry, to be unable to pay for school, and to live in decrepit conditions. In spite of the darkness that surrounded me in my youth, I always remained focused on a single light, the dream of rising out of the pervasive misery that surrounded me. I knew education was my primary gateway to a better life. I thus devoted myself academically so as to graduate from high school, and earned a coveted spot among the few to be admitted to the Faculty of Sciences at the State University of Haiti."

Nonetheless, he understands now he has a responsibility toward his nation. The problem that he went through as a child helps him to define his purpose that he turns into a

Triumphing Over Hell On Earth

vision. He presented his vision to transform Haiti Socio-Economic status with three pillars:

1. **Quality education for all Haitians:** No Haitian should be condemned by his or her social background, skin color, or place of birth (*OrijinMwen pa kaKondane'm*, My Origins Cannot Condemn Me).
2. **Economic decentralization:** The delegation of power to minimize the control of the few over the economy, and to give true power to both the people and to the local communities.
3. **A strong institutional framework:** The establishment of necessary institutions to uphold the rule of law and pave the way for political stability.

These are great ideas, but our Creator's plan is the most reliable one because He is the source. If your source is right your fruit will also be right, but if your source has problem then you will have problem as well. Presidential candidates, regardless of the country in which they are running, always frame their political agenda on basic human needs because they know we are relying on these items. They use our basic human needs as a platform - a need that should have never been a need, according to the Creator's plan.

You now understand that basic human needs such as food, water, clothes, and shelter should not be your worries. You have now rediscovered that you have access to everything that you need to become yourself. You have now been taught that you should seek first His kingdom and

Planning

His righteousness and everything else will come along including your purpose.

The final step is to create a plan based on the information received from the self-discovery questionnaire you have created. This planning is the blueprint of your future. In this planning, you need to write down all the steps you will need to take in order to achieve your goal, because success is the product of many well-planned little steps. For example, what are the resources that you need to achieve your goal? Where can you get these resources? How long would it take to achieve the first step? You need to take the time to write the necessary steps needed to achieve the goals that you listed in your plan.

It can be a tedious process, yet extremely beneficial for the end result. For example, if one of the goals is to go back to school, then you have to research the school's requirements, the tuition, and the time frame. These are the kinds of thinking that can lead you to achieve all the goals that you have listed in your plan.

Remember, the plan is a starting point. It is simply a design container to hold your ideas and the steps to attend your purpose; therefore as your purpose begins to develop, to shape, and define, it may require some alteration in the plan. It is similar to building a house; the ultimate goal of the architect is to design the house, which requires a blueprint to guide the process. Many times the engineers have to modify the blueprint in order to meet the standard codes of housing. The ultimate goal is like building the house, the process of modification does not deviate. Rather it improves the security of completing the house safely.

Your plan is a bridge to help you cross over successfully. It can be revised and refined as you see fit. Again, identifying the purpose of your journey can be beneficial. With proper planning you can achieve your purpose. With proper planning we can change the world, we can end hunger, we can design a water plant, and we can develop all the materials and fabrics to design clothes, and to build houses for the world.

Our Creator gave us all the tools we need to be successful. He created us to become world changers. He created a plan for our life that allows us to share His mighty work of creation, remember, He gave us His image, His character, and His abilities to do great work and He also gave us free will, but He tells us: if we plan, He will provide the resources for our vision.

Planning

Key Principles:

1. Planning should be the first thing you think about.
2. Planning makes vision possible.
3. A well-balanced plan will help you to prioritize your life.
4. A plan will set you apart from mediocrity to superiority.
5. It is important to understand your purpose in order to have a successful vision.
6. A purposeful educational plan is the gateway for a successful life.

Triumphing Over Hell On Earth

Chapter 11

HOW TO WRITE YOUR VISION

Proper planning is an essential component to your success. As you may now understand, we are created with a purpose and we are given a vision of how it will be fulfilled according to our Creator's expectations for us. Our Creator designated us with potentials, gifts, and talents to accomplish our purpose and to make our vision a reality. Basic human needs are not to be a concern. Instead we must have big dreams and we should see farther than our eyes can look for ourselves, our community, and our nations. Below is how you can begin the process of writing your vision and how you can obtain the result that you need to be successful. **Proverbs 16:1** tells us "To man belong the plans of the heart, but from the Lord comes the proper answer of the tongue."[61] This verse reiterates the importance of creating a plan in order to see our vision prosper. Also in Hebrew the words heart and mind are synonymous. So the above verse tells us that plans come from man's heart, it is therefore from the mind.

Writing a plan transcribes what is in your mind therefore from your heart. This is also your first action step in getting

---

[61] Proverbs 16:1

your plans in motion. Once you write your plans, you make them clear.

In the previous chapter you had the opportunity to answer the eleven-questions to discover yourself. Now you have the 8 steps to write your vision. I encourage you to have fun with it and allow the process to lead your journey to discover your purpose, and transform it into a vision.

Writing Your Vision: 8 Steps

Step 1: Eliminate Distractions
Sit down somewhere by yourself, away from any distractions and responsibilities, and allow yourself some uninterrupted time to think. Do this as often as you need as you develop your plan.

Step 2: Find Your True Self
Until you know who you are, why God created you, and why you're here, life will simply be a confusing experiment. Answering the following questions will help give you clarity and confidence with regard to your personal identity.
- Who am I?
- Who am I in relation to God?
- Where do I come from as a person?
- How have I been created like my Source? (see Genesis 1:26-28)
- Why am I here?

Write out your personal purpose statement. Ask yourself, "What is my reason for existence as a human being and as an individual?" (You may be able to answer this question only after you have completed the other steps. However, you may also want to write an answer now and then compare it with what you think after you have gone through the rest of the questions.)

Step 3: Find Your True Vision

Answer the following questions, and you'll be amazed at the way God will begin to open your mind to His purpose and vision for you. You'll begin to see things that you've never seen before. Put them down on paper, read them over, think about them, pray about them, and begin to formulate ideas of what you want out of life. Ask yourself the following:

- What do I want to do with my life?
- What am I inspired to do?
- What would I want to do more than anything else, even if I was never paid for it?
- What do I love to do so much that I forget to eat or sleep?

Allow yourself to think freely. Don't put any limitations of time or money on your vision. Because many of us are influenced by others' opinions of us and by our own false expectations for ourselves, it may take you a little time to discover what you really want. Persevere through the process and dig down deep to find your true desires. Below are activities to help you do this.

Step 4: Discover Your True Motivation

A vision from God is never selfish. It will always help or uplift others in some way. It is designed to make the lives of humankind better and to improve society. It inspires and builds up others. Ask yourself the following:

- How does my vision help others?
- What is the motivation for my vision?
- Why do I want to do what I want to do?
- Can I accomplish my vision and still have integrity?

Step 5: Identify Your Principles

Your principles are your philosophy of life. In other words, they are how you intend to conduct yourself during your life. You must clarify what you will and won't do. These principles are your guides for living, doing business, relating to other people, and relating to life. You must settle them in your heart and mind so that you will have standards to live by. The Ten Commandments are great principles and a good starting point for developing your own principles. For example, you could write, "On my way to my vision, I will not steal, lie, or bear false witness. I won't worship any god but God the Father. I will not commit adultery. I will not covet and so on."

- Write down your life principles.

Step 6: Choose Your Goals and Objectives

Goals are the steps necessary to fulfill your vision. What practical things do you need to do to accomplish your dream? Goals are clear markers that will take you where you need to go.

- Write out your goals.

Objectives are the detailed steps of your goals. They determine when you want things to happen. You must clearly delineate what you need to do and when you need to do it in order to get to where you want to go. For example, if you want to open a mechanics shop, and one of your goals is to go to school to learn mechanics, some of your objectives will be to choose a school, fill out an application, and start classes. Objectives should include specific timetables.

- Write down your objectives.

Step 7: Identify Your Resources

You now need to identify all the resources you will need to accomplish your vision.

- *Identify your human needs.*

What help do you need from others to fulfill your vision? What kind of personal associations do you need to have – and not have?

- *Identify your resource needs.*

How To Write Your Vision

What kinds of resources do you need to fulfill your vision? Don't worry about how large they may seem. Write them down.
- *Write down your strengths.*

Who are you? What are your gifts? What do you know you are good at? Write down your answers, and then make plans to refine your strengths. For example, if your vision requires that you have to speak before large groups of people, you have to start stepping out and doing it. You are probably going to be scared at first, yet God will give you opportunities to speak at different stages so you can develop your gift. You don't even know what you can do until you have to. Some amazing gifts come out of people when they are under pressure.
- Write down your weaknesses.

What does your vision need that you aren't good at? Don't be ashamed of your weaknesses, because everyone has something they are not good at. You don't have the monopoly on that. However, you must identify them because God will supply other people to do what you cannot do toward your vision. You need other people in your life because your vision cannot be fulfilled by you alone.

Step 8: Commit to Your Vision

You will never fulfill your vision if you are not committed to it. You will need to make a specific decision that you are going to follow through with what you want to do, acknowledging that God may refine your plans as He leads you through the process. Also, commit your vision to God on a regular basis. Proverbs 16:3 says "Commit to the Lord whatever you do, and your plans will succeed."
- Commit to your vision.
- Commit your vision to God.

Key Principles

1. Planning requires a process.
2. Planning will give meaning to your vision.
3. A well-balanced plan will help you to prioritize your life.
4. If you want progress you must have a plan.
5. Failure is predictable just like success is predictable.
6. Knowledge in any form is power.
7. Education leads to knowledge.

Chapter 12

TIME FOR A CHANGE

Complete access, not ownership is the life style that reflects the King's culture

People around the world are struggling to meet their simple human basic needs: food, water, clothing, and housing. This problem is very obvious in our culture, in our daily lives, in our community, regardless of our nationalities, skin colors, and religious affiliations. People risk their lives and family with the hope that one day it will get better. We migrate from place to place without realizing we carry the same problems as well as the tools to solve the problems but because we are so focused on the problems we neglect to explore the potential that is inside us. The talents, the gifts, the creativity that our Creator carefully placed within us are just so we can design the next water system, to become the next leader in the agricultural world, to become the next top designer, and absolutely the next top engineer who will build houses all over the world. But there are two principles to apply: The first one is to seek His Kingdom and the second one is to be in right standing. Simple enough for us to put in application, I would say! God challenges us to compare our

Triumphing Over Hell On Earth

needs to the birds and reminds us how the birds never once go without a meal yet they don't sow. He promised to do the very same thing for us but we have to have faith and believe it can be done.

Faith is the measurement God uses to assess our belief in His promise system that He created for us. Imagine yourself as a citizen in good standing. You are a good citizen of your country. You respect the laws of the land. You follow the rules that are in place and you understand they were created just to keep you safe, therefore you live with no worry knowing that you have a reliable government that will take care of you as long as you remain righteous.

It is the same for our King. As long as we follow His Divine laws and principles we are in accordance. According to **Joshua 1:8 we must** "Keep this Book of the Law always on your lips; meditate on it day and night, so that you may be careful to do everything written in it. Then you will be prosperous and successful."[62] The reasons why the same problem keeps reoccurring are because we are the solvers, and we don't understand the kingdom governing system, which was the original plan. God wanted earth to be a replica of heaven. He has two kingdoms: kingdom of heaven and kingdom of earth using the same rules, same concepts, same laws, and same principles. "I will give you the keys of the kingdom of heaven; whatever you bind on earth will be bound in heaven, and whatever you lose on

---

[62] Joshua 1:8

Time For A Change

earth will be lost in heaven."[63] Until we take the time to evaluate ourselves we will always be in need unless we stop, think, and reflect.

Stop repeating the same steps. As you can see, they are not working. You have been trying for the longest time. It is time to try something new, a rediscovering, or a transformation of the mind.

I had the privilege of attending two Haitian presidential debates for the 2016 election. One hosted by the National Association of Haitian Professionals (NAHP) in Washington DC and the other by Friends of Haiti 2010 (FOH 2010) in North Miami. I was very impressed to see and hear all the candidates who were in attendance. They all agreed that the Haitian people need a transformation of the mind in order for Haiti to move forward. I also believe that the Haitian people must choose a different way of thinking. According to the original plan of the Creator they need to think differently. They need to believe that they are able people and capable of doing "all things through Christ who strengthens"[64] them to change the situation that the country of Haiti has been enduring for the past 40 plus years. They need to take responsibility for themselves. They cannot rely on their government, their neighbors, their family and their friends. I was concerned that the candidates did not talk about the "How" the people could receive that mind transformation that is gravely needed to save the nation.

---

[63] Matthew 16: 19
[64] Philippians 4:13

The candidates also spent a large amount of time talking about the gravity of the agricultural system in Haiti.

The more I listened to them the more I could see how they were magnifying the problem amongst them on the podium. I came to the conclusion that they don't have the solution either because they were going about it the wrong way. They understood the "what" but couldn't answer the "how." Our Creator warned us not to worry about what we will eat and yet we are having a presidential debate based on that same warning.

No wonder Haiti's economic system can't move forward. The source is wrong. The foundation is wrong. The Constitution, which is the back-bone of the country, is out of order. It is out of order because the fundamental element is missing. The original plan of our Creator has not been acknowledged. They are operating in a democratic system, which encourages ownership that creates stress and dilemmas. Kragh explains the effect of ownership, "It creates frustration, depression, lack, theft, scarcity, stress and has limitations." Haiti's ownership system is not as powerful as America's due to lack of opportunities. Nonetheless, every Haitian person wants to own something regardless of how it is owned. This concept is devouring the nations because ownership is a curse. Our Creator wants us to have access not ownership.

Ownership comes with responsibility to keep up with the fixation of the accumulated obligations. "The more things we accumulate, the more money it takes to maintain them."

Time For A Change

I was always questioning myself about people who work very hard to own a house with a beautiful landscaping and within a few years the landscape image keeps fading away. They can't maintain the ownership obligation. It would have been better to have access. In Haiti everyone owns a "house." It is mainly a shack but they want to become owners. The Haitian candidates talked about the failure of the education system in Haiti where 80 percent of the schools are privately own, yet can't sustain the ownership protocol due to lack of resources. According to Dr. Munroe resources are:

1. People
2. Experience
3. Relationships
4. Energy
5. Monetary

Most people focus only on number 5, monetary, (worry) ignoring the other four factors in addition to the most important factor, God, who is the ultimate source for all that we need because He created them all for our benefit.

How do we make that operational transition that can transform our lives for the better? The key is to understand the economic system of God in comparison to our earthly economic system in order to avoid toiling. According to God toiling is a curse. In the Garden of Eden toiling did not exist. Adam had complete access to everything that he needed until he disobeyed his Creator. In the kingdom of God we have commonwealth and we use the currency of faith.

Commonwealth

In order to truly understand this concept you need to deprogram your mind. This is where the transformation becomes vital. In God's country commonwealth is the norm. Where there is commonwealth the King has obligation toward His citizens' welfare. In that country there is always an overflow of resources (people, experience, time, relationships, energy, and money) accessible to the citizens. Equality is well defined in His country. You and I have equal amount of health, time, money, energy, guidance, and protection. Lordship is also a very important principle to understand. "Jesus is Lord" is a very common phrase. Jesus was given the name Lord that means ADONI or owner. So when we say "Jesus is Lord" we are basically saying "Jesus is the owner." The owner of what? Everything, all of our resources that we need to become Jesus, also refers to Himself as the King. Again, the King owns everything and gives His citizens complete access to all His resources. Adam had complete access in the Garden of Eden. God told Adam in Genesis 2 " You are free to eat from any tree in the gardens." Nothing was off limit, very different in comparison to the democratic world. In the democratic system, people want to limit your capacity, they want to distribute the wealth and most of the time they want total ownership and leave you with nothing.

Currency

In any government system, in order to conduct business, there must be a form of currency in place. For example, in Haiti we have the currency of Gourde, in America we have the Dollar, and most of the European countries utilize the Euro. Currency is so important that if you want to travel to other countries you must know the currency system that is being used so you can exchange your country's currency to theirs.

In the kingdom faith is the currency that is used. In order to conduct transaction with your King you have to have the right currency.

What is Faith?

Faith is the ability to believe in things that you can't see or not even knowing how it can happen. It is the ability to hope. Without hope there is no purpose. Belief is the source of reason for commitment, for persistence, for tenacity. We need both faith and belief. I learned that when "belief is lost then life has no expectation, and the greatest loss in life on earth is the loss of belief." Hebrew 11:1 tells us that "Now faith is the substance of things hoped for, the evidence of things not seen."[65] In order to have access to God we have to believe that He is relevant, that He is present. We also have to understand and believe in the kingdom government just like Isaiah proclaimed and prophesized, "For to us a child is born to us a son is given, and the

---

65 Hebrew 11: 1

Triumphing Over Hell On Earth

government will be on his shoulders. And he will be called Wonderful Counselor, Mighty God, Everlasting Father, Prince of Peace."[66] As kingdom citizens we have the right to make transactions with God, but without the proper currency (faith) we have no access to Him and all His promises. "I will give you the key of the kingdom of heaven whatever you lose on earth will be lost in heaven."[67] A full conviction is that God will function in our lives today and in the future, even when we don't comprehend why it is necessary. **Roman 8: 24-25** "...hope that is see is no hope at all, because who hopes for what he already has. We hope for what we don't see and wait patiently for it, because we know that it is coming."[68] Faith gives us access to all His rights, privileges, and His benefits which is why being a citizen of this country is a lifestyle, it cannot be a hobby, and it cannot be a fad. We have to have the character traits of our King because He allows us to have access to His Kingdom all the time.

If we want total access to the commonwealth of God we must have faith and believe in all His Divine Laws and Principles. Faith drives us to take action. We must do the work to make it relevant. **James 2:26** tells us that "Faith without work is dead."[69] In the kingdom we pay tithe, it is 10% taxation on what you make, just like you pay taxes to your government. Taxes have to be paid in the kingdom of God as well. If you don't pay your taxes in America you will get in trouble with the law. It is also the same in the kingdom.

---

66 Isaiah 9:6
67 Matthew 6:19
68 Roman 8: 24-25
69 James 2: 26

Time For A Change

If you want to maintain your rights and remain in good standing with your king you need to meet your obligation. Kragh emphasized in her book *Figure it out* that paying tithe is not for prosperity, it is the right thing to do. Good citizens have rights and they are able to exercise their rights and most importantly, their government has an obligation toward them. This is how Malachi explains it:

"Will a man rob God? Yet you have robbed me! But you say, 'In what way have we robbed You?' In tithes and offerings. You are cursed with a curse. For you have robbed Me, even this whole nation. Bring all the tithes into the storehouse. That there may be food in My house, And try Me now in this," Says the Lord of hosts, "If I will not open for you the windows of heaven and pour out for you such blessing that there will not be room enough to receive it."[70]

Windows in Hebrew is an idiom for access. He will give you access to unseen resources if you pay your taxes (tithes). This activates the economy system of the government of God. "The earth is the LORD's, and everything in it, the world, and all who live in it."

The Haitian government system may not be resourceful enough which explains the scarcity for simple basic human needs, but Haiti belongs to God and everything on earth belongs to God. He is able to give Haiti all the necessary resources to become functional just like any other nations.

---

[70] Malachi 3: 8-10

Triumphing Over Hell On Earth

The people of Haiti, however, have to meet these guidelines: seek first His kingdom and His righteousness; conform to His Divine Laws and Principles; and understand the Kingdom government's economic system. Because of the democratic system the people are used to "ownership." Unfortunately, in the kingdom, ownership tied the hands of God from pouring all His blessing based on this list:

- The spirit of ownership creates limitation.
- The spirit of ownership creates frustration.
- The spirit of ownership creates depression.
- The spirit of ownership creates contention.
- The spirit of ownership creates scarcity.
- The spirit of ownership creates lack.
- The spirit of ownership creates stealing.
- The spirit of ownership creates poverty.
- The spirit of ownership creates stress.
- The spirit of ownership creates sickness and death.

I remember talking to Candidate Mathias Pierre. He was sharing with me how hungry the people of Haiti are. I saw the sadness in his eyes and in his voice because he has so much love and desire to transform the country, but the people's minds have to be transformed first because they have all the solutions that Haiti needs to get out of poverty. They just don't know it yet.

Why such scarcity? How did we get to be so desperate? We are working day and night just to live and living to work. We have decided that we can do all things, and all things depend on us. Because our mindsets are wrong, our lives will

Time For A Change

If you want to maintain your rights and remain in good standing with your king you need to meet your obligation. Kragh emphasized in her book *Figure it out* that paying tithe is not for prosperity, it is the right thing to do. Good citizens have rights and they are able to exercise their rights and most importantly, their government has an obligation toward them. This is how Malachi explains it:

"Will a man rob God? Yet you have robbed me! But you say, 'In what way have we robbed You?' In tithes and offerings. You are cursed with a curse. For you have robbed Me, even this whole nation. Bring all the tithes into the storehouse. That there may be food in My house, And try Me now in this," Says the Lord of hosts, "If I will not open for you the windows of heaven and pour out for you such blessing that there will not be room enough to receive it."[70]

Windows in Hebrew is an idiom for access. He will give you access to unseen resources if you pay your taxes (tithes). This activates the economy system of the government of God. "The earth is the LORD's, and everything in it, the world, and all who live in it."

The Haitian government system may not be resourceful enough which explains the scarcity for simple basic human needs, but Haiti belongs to God and everything on earth belongs to God. He is able to give Haiti all the necessary resources to become functional just like any other nations.

---

[70] Malachi 3: 8-10

Triumphing Over Hell On Earth

The people of Haiti, however, have to meet these guidelines: seek first His kingdom and His righteousness; conform to His Divine Laws and Principles; and understand the Kingdom government's economic system. Because of the democratic system the people are used to "ownership." Unfortunately, in the kingdom, ownership tied the hands of God from pouring all His blessing based on this list:

- The spirit of ownership creates limitation.
- The spirit of ownership creates frustration.
- The spirit of ownership creates depression.
- The spirit of ownership creates contention.
- The spirit of ownership creates scarcity.
- The spirit of ownership creates lack.
- The spirit of ownership creates stealing.
- The spirit of ownership creates poverty.
- The spirit of ownership creates stress.
- The spirit of ownership creates sickness and death.

I remember talking to Candidate Mathias Pierre. He was sharing with me how hungry the people of Haiti are. I saw the sadness in his eyes and in his voice because he has so much love and desire to transform the country, but the people's minds have to be transformed first because they have all the solutions that Haiti needs to get out of poverty. They just don't know it yet.

Why such scarcity? How did we get to be so desperate? We are working day and night just to live and living to work. We have decided that we can do all things, and all things depend on us. Because our mindsets are wrong, our lives will

Time For A Change

also be wrong. We were created to do even greater things than our Creator. His desire for us! "Very truly I tell you, whoever believes in me will do the works I have been doing, and they will do even greater things than these..."[71]

Inside of each one of us are dormant gifts, talents, potentials, purpose, and vision. We have lost the sense of the original plan the Creator had for us. We have, therefore, adapted a lifestyle that started in Genesis chapter 3 after the rebellion of Adam and Eve as Kragh stated in her book *Figure it out.*

This is how God expressed his anger toward Adam, "Cursed is the ground because of you; through painful toil you will eat food from it all the days of your life." We are still being impacted by the fall of man although we have been redeemed by the Master Teacher Jesus to the original plan of God described in **Genesis chapters 1 and 2**. As Trista Kragh explained the redemption process, "The curse happened in **Genesis chapter 3** and the remainder of the Bible is a repair program to get us back to the first two chapters of Genesis where it all started in the Garden of Eden." I am sure most of the political candidates would like to offer the Haitian people a "Garden of Eden" but they don't know how, which explains why president after president the poverty level of Haiti is getting deeper and deeper. A new mindset is what is needed. It is reassuring to know that if God gives an assignment, He always provides the resources and He places them at our disposal to utilize.

---

[71] John 14:12

Triumphing Over Hell On Earth

My late mentor Dr. Munroe helped the Visionary group to produce a song titled "Brand New World." Below are the lyrics to the song.

"Brand New World" by Artist: Derek Flowers
www.GodlyChristianMusic.com

> We don't like the way the world is turning
> Something inside is always yearning, yearning for a
> Brand New World
> People everywhere are so confused
> Leaders don't know what to do.
>
> Oh, how we want a Brand New World.
> Though we send rockets to the moon and the stars
> And though we make ships and planes that go very far
> There's not a mountain that man hasn't climbed
> But a Brand New World he can never find
>
> So if you want a Brand New World you gotta have brand new people
> And if you want brand new people you gotta have a brand new life, oh
>
> And if you want a brand new life you gotta have a brand new spirit
> And if you want a brand new spirit you gotta come to Jesus Christ. Yeah, yeah
>
> People have tried everything they could

But I wonder if they ever would
Find themselves a brand new world.
An old man sitting in the bar room door
Still can't find what he's searching for,

Oh how he wants a brand new world.
A brand new world begins with me and you
But we'll never find it in the things that we do
Jesus promised a world that's our own
And He invites us to come along

So if you want a Brand New World you gotta have brand new people
And if you want brand new people you gotta have a brand new life
And if you want a brand new life you gotta have a brand new spirit
And if you want a brand new spirit you gotta come to Jesus Christ.

I believe this is what Haiti needs, new people, with a new mindset to change things around. This is something we all can benefit from as well.

I hope this book helps you understand that life is not just about satisfying basic human needs, but that seeking His kingdom and His righteousness is far more important because it removes the human's complexity for doing things. It gives us keys and life principles on how to live life to the fullest according to the plan that He created for us. It helps us to find our purpose and vision, something that each one of us was born with, and somehow managed to let life's obstacles take away from us.

This book is a symbol to remind you that you are worth more than you think you can achieve, and more than what you have achieved in the past. As Dr. Munroe would say, "Your potential is much greater than what you are right now. What you will become is much more than you could ever imagine or believe." I have learned that it may take tenacity, audacity, and courage to transform a purpose into a vision. Most importantly, it takes the understanding of what we lost though the fall of man and how we can regain control if we apply these two requests made by our creator. "First seek His kingdom and His righteousness." I had had the opportunity to interact with people who had demonstrated such qualities. For example, my late mentor Dr. Munroe had devoted forty plus years of his life to pursue his purpose a profoundly needed knowledge to change the world. He believed that the Bible was not being taught as it was supposed to which had created more confusion in the religious world. He chose to reteach the mission of Jesus' "First seek His kingdom and His righteousness."

He believed if we understood the teaching of Jesus we would understand then what we had lost through the fall of man. We had lost the kingdom, the dominion, the control, and the power that God gave us in **Genesis 1:26.** Dr. Munroe had transformed his purpose into a vision by "Transforming Followers Into Leaders And Leaders Into Agents Of Change." Kragh also made a sacrifice by devoting to live her life based on Divine Laws and Principles in order to

But I wonder if they ever would
Find themselves a brand new world.
An old man sitting in the bar room door
Still can't find what he's searching for,

Oh how he wants a brand new world.
A brand new world begins with me and you
But we'll never find it in the things that we do
Jesus promised a world that's our own
And He invites us to come along

So if you want a Brand New World you gotta have brand new people
And if you want brand new people you gotta have a brand new life
And if you want a brand new life you gotta have a brand new spirit
And if you want a brand new spirit you gotta come to Jesus Christ.

I believe this is what Haiti needs, new people, with a new mindset to change things around. This is something we all can benefit from as well.

I hope this book helps you understand that life is not just about satisfying basic human needs, but that seeking His kingdom and His righteousness is far more important because it removes the human's complexity for doing things. It gives us keys and life principles on how to live life to the fullest according to the plan that He created for us. It helps us to find our purpose and vision, something that each

Triumphing Over Hell On Earth

one of us was born with, and somehow managed to let life's obstacles take away from us.

This book is a symbol to remind you that you are worth more than you think you can achieve, and more than what you have achieved in the past. As Dr. Munroe would say, "Your potential is much greater than what you are right now. What you will become is much more than you could ever imagine or believe." I have learned that it may take tenacity, audacity, and courage to transform a purpose into a vision. Most importantly, it takes the understanding of what we lost though the fall of man and how we can regain control if we apply these two requests made by our creator. "First seek His kingdom and His righteousness." I had had the opportunity to interact with people who had demonstrated such qualities. For example, my late mentor Dr. Munroe had devoted forty plus years of his life to pursue his purpose a profoundly needed knowledge to change the world. He believed that the Bible was not being taught as it was supposed to which had created more confusion in the religious world. He chose to reteach the mission of Jesus' "First seek His kingdom and His righteousness."

He believed if we understood the teaching of Jesus we would understand then what we had lost through the fall of man. We had lost the kingdom, the dominion, the control, and the power that God gave us in **Genesis 1:26.** Dr. Munroe had transformed his purpose into a vision by "Transforming Followers Into Leaders And Leaders Into Agents Of Change." Kragh also made a sacrifice by devoting to live her life based on Divine Laws and Principles in order to

Time For A Change

reflect the culture of her King. That lifestyle had taken her to many nations: Lebanon, India, Turkey, and Indonesia teaching, others how to find their purpose and passion in order to live a purposeful life through kingdom principles. My dear pastor friend had also devoted her life to serve her community by creating many profound giving ministries in Immokalee Florida which recognized her among many other pastors and community leaders, which is why I cant wait for her to understand what was the purpose of Jesus' mission. Jesus only taught one message: the kingdom. A message that is so critical in order to regain access of our birth's rights through faith.

I also admire the courage of all the Haitian Candidates I saw at second Haitian presidential debate in North Miami Senior High school and the one from D.C to believe that they can make a difference in the youth of Haiti. They believe that they have the remedy to calm the hunger pain that they see everyday on the streets of Port-au-Prince.

Because I read some of their proposals (plans) I came to believe that they could bring the change that Haiti needs. It may take some time but it is hopeful to see some people are willing to let go of their comfort and fight for the voiceless with the hope that the youth will be able to discover their purpose in life and in return they can help Haiti make the change that is so necessary.

A change is what it will take to help you "seek first His kingdom and His righteousness" to help you discover yourself, find your purpose, write a plan and transform it into a vision by applying His commonwealth economic system through your faith. If we can grasp His Divine Laws and Principles we would not have to worry about food, water, clothes, and shelter. The Bible tells us that life is far more important than stressing about basic human needs, we are encouraged instead to believe and have faith knowing that the earth is His and everything in the world belongs to Him. We are His children He will never forsake us. He knows what we need. Our responsibility is to remain obedient and live our life through His standards measured by the life keys that He gave us. We are more than enough and we were created with purpose, gifts, talents, abilities, capacities, and intelligent to become.

Cannon Farrar wrote:
I am only one
But I am one
I cannot do everything
But I can do something
What I can do
I ought to do
And what I ought to do
By the grace of God.

I encourage you to find your purpose and make a vision out of it, one step at a time, but leave big prints behind.

Key Principles:

1. Planning is critical to your success.
2. We were created with hidden treasures that are still dormant, waiting to be discovered.
3. Your vision is the by-product of your vision.
4. Your vision is for the benefit of thee next generation.
5. Your Creator will supply people to do what you cannot do for your vision.

APPENDIX

The Kingdom of God Ambassador's Pledge

"I confess Jesus Christ as my Lord, my Savior, my Redeemer, and my King.
I accept the Holy Spirit, the Governor of Heaven, to live in me now, forever.
I accept the word of God as my Constitution and the Laws of this Constitution, and I pledge to obey them until I die.
I receive the mandate to go into all the world and take the gospel of the kingdom of God into every nation, every system, and every neighborhood.
I receive this solemn pledge, and I will not violate the laws of God.
I will obey my King without question.
Amen."

Because of your confession, I confer on you in the Name of the Father, Son, and the Holy Spirit, the Ambassadorial credentials of the kingdom of Heaven.
May He put upon your shoulders, His sword; and knight you as Kings and Priests upon the earth.
May you walk boldly without fear.
May you never be afraid of the eyes of those who look at you, for you are the great one.
He who is in you is greater than he who is in the world.
He who is in you is greater than He who is in the world.
He who is in you is greater than he who is in the world.
Therefore, go boldly and declare the kingdom of God.
And lo, I am with you always even unto the end of this age, and no man shall stand before you.

Today, you are pledged to be God's Amassador.
Represent the Kingdom well and be afraid of nothing, for the LORD is with you.
And if the LORD is with you, who can be against you?
Today, you have been transformed.

Recommended Readings

- Gospels of Matthew, Mark, Luke and John seven times.
- *Rediscovering the Kingdom* – Dr. Myles Munroe
- *The Most Important Person on Earth* – Dr. Myles Munroe
- *The Principles and Power of Vision* – Dr. Myles Munroe
- *Re-discovering Faith* – Dr. Myles Munroe
- *Overcoming Crisis* – Dr. Myles Munroe

About the Author

Dr. Juniace Senecharles Etienne is currently a French teacher with the Collier Public Schools in Naples, Florida. Dr. Etienne works with children at all academic skill levels; from those with special needs to those who are academically gifted. In addition to teaching, Dr. Etienne has written, *Three Steps to Guide Your Children's Educational Future*.

She is also an international speaker and educational consultant. Recent lecture topics include: *Goals Setting; Prioritizing for a Successful High School Experience, Preparing for a Successful Parent/Teacher Conference, Preparing our 21st Century Student for Academic Success* and *Planning for Life after High School*. She is currently the lead campaign coordinator in the United States for Haiti's 2015 presidential election.

Dr. Etienne graduated Summa Cum Laude from Barry University, received her master's degree in Reading from Nova Southern University, and earned her doctoral degree in Teacher Leadership from Walden University. She is married to Romel Etienne and is the mother of two wonderful daughters: Joyce, Jessica, Samantha, and Sheena.

As a native of Miragôane, Haiti, who migrated to the United States at the age of 16, Dr. Etienne knows firsthand that education can expand one's opportunities to succeed. Her passion is to empower and stimulate intellectual curiosity in her students. Her goal is to inform world leaders about the importance of accessible education and its necessity in creating a stronger future for our children.

Recommended Readings

- Gospels of Matthew, Mark, Luke and John seven times.
- *Rediscovering the Kingdom* – Dr. Myles Munroe
- *The Most Important Person on Earth* – Dr. Myles Munroe
- *The Principles and Power of Vision* – Dr. Myles Munroe
- *Re-discovering Faith* – Dr. Myles Munroe
- *Overcoming Crisis* – Dr. Myles Munroe

Triumphing Over Hell On Earth

About the Author

Dr. Juniace Senecharles Etienne is currently a French teacher with the Collier Public Schools in Naples, Florida. Dr. Etienne works with children at all academic skill levels; from those with special needs to those who are academically gifted. In addition to teaching, Dr. Etienne has written, *Three Steps to Guide Your Children's Educational Future.*

She is also an international speaker and educational consultant. Recent lecture topics include: *Goals Setting; Prioritizing for a Successful High School Experience, Preparing for a Successful Parent/Teacher Conference, Preparing our 21st Century Student for Academic Success* and *Planning for Life after High School.* She is currently the lead campaign coordinator in the United States for Haiti's 2015 presidential election.

Dr. Etienne graduated Summa Cum Laude from Barry University, received her master's degree in Reading from Nova Southern University, and earned her doctoral degree in Teacher Leadership from Walden University. She is married to Romel Etienne and is the mother of two wonderful daughters: Joyce, Jessica, Samantha, and Sheena.

As a native of Miragôane, Haiti, who migrated to the United States at the age of 16, Dr. Etienne knows firsthand that education can expand one's opportunities to succeed. Her passion is to empower and stimulate intellectual curiosity in her students. Her goal is to inform world leaders about the importance of accessible education and its necessity in creating a stronger future for our children.

Other Works by the Author

- A Grounded Theory Approach to Use of Differentiate Instruction to Improve Students' Outcomes in Mathematics

- Three Steps To Guide Your Children Educational Future

REFERENCES

- Darfur refugee camp in Chad
- Etienne, S. J. (2015). Three Steps T Guide Your Children Educational.
- Financingthefuture.com
- http://en.wikipedia.org/wiki/File:Darfur_refugee_camp_in_Chad.jpg / CC BY-SA
- http://ncowie.files.wordpress.com/2010/07/biafra-fidelvasquez.jpg Original URL: http://ncowie.wordpress.com/page/35/
- http://www.flickr.com/photos/un_photo/4421127032/sizes/o/
- https://en.wikipedia.org/wiki/**Frederic_Farrar**
- https://en.wikipedia.org/wiki/Vapor
- https://www.biblegateway.com/passage/?search=
- https://www.e-education.psu.edu/earth103/node/806
- https://www.eeducation.psu.edu/earth103/files/earth103/module09/Florida_chicken_house.jpg
- https://www.eeducation.psu.edu/earth103/files/earth103/module09/IndiaFarm.jpg
- Kragh, T.S. (2010). How to write your personal vision.[Newsletter Article]. Article from Kingdom Connection Newsletter. Naples, FL: www.TristaSue.com
- Kragh, T.S. (2015). Figure it out. Maverick Production.
- Munroe, M. (2003). The principles and power of vision: keys to achieving personal and corporate destiny. New Kensington,PA: Whitaker House.

Triumphing Over Hell On Earth

- Munroe, M. (2003). Understand Your Potential. Discovering the Hidden You. Destiny Image Publishers, Inc.
- WDTN.com, police in Miami Township
- Work found at http://en.wikipedia.org/wiki/Day_of_Seven_Billion / CC BY-SA 3.0 (http://creativecommons.org/licenses/by-sa/3.0/)
- www.weforum.org/social.../**kamal-quadir**: Bkask kamal quasir

Made in the USA
Charleston, SC
31 December 2015